AQA (A) GCSE
SCHOOLS HISTORY PROJECT

SECOND EDITION

J A Cloake
L Pellow
P M Johnson

HODDER
EDUCATION
AN HACHETTE UK COMPANY

The Publishers would like to thank the following for permission to reproduce copyright material:

Photo credits P.13 © PARIS PIERCE / Alamy; **p.28** © The Trustees of the British Museum; **p.30** © DEA / A. DAGLI ORTI / Getty Images; **p.45** *l* © James Kratz – Fotolia, *r* © 2002 Topham / Fotomas / TopFoto; **p.46** © 2002 Topham / Fotomas / TopFoto; **p.72** © SuperStock; **p.77** © The Granger Collection, NYC/TopFoto; **p.78** © Pioneer's home in the American wilderness, 1867 (colour litho), Palmer, Frances Flora Bond (Fanny) (c.1812–76) / Private Collection / Peter Newark American Pictures / The Bridgeman Art Library; **p.79** © Pioneer woman collecting cattle dung, Kansas, c.1880 (coloured photo), American Photographer, (19th century) / Private Collection / Peter Newark Western Americana / The Bridgeman Art Library; **p.83** © The Granger Collection, NYC/TopFoto; **p.91** © WOOLAROC MUSEUM, BARTLESVILLE, OKLAHOMA; **p.97** © Matwijow, Klaus / Süddeutsche Zeitung Photo; **p.98** © Ullstein Bild / TopFoto; **p.110** © Mary Evans Picture Library/WEIMAR ARCHIVE; **p.114** © World History Archive / TopFoto; **p.115** © Mary Evans / Sueddeutsche Zeitung Photo; **p.117** © The Granger Collection / TopFoto; **p.122** © akg-images.

AQA material is reproduced by permission of AQA. Solutions and commentaries for exam practice questions have not been provided by or approved by AQA and they may not necessarily constitute the only possible solutions.

Every effort has been made to trace all copyright holders, but if any have been inadvertently overlooked the Publishers will be pleased to make the necessary arrangements at the first opportunity.

Although every effort has been made to ensure that website addresses are correct at time of going to press, Hodder Education cannot be held responsible for the content of any website mentioned in this book. It is sometimes possible to find a relocated web page by typing in the address of the home page for a website in the URL window of your browser.

Hachette UK's policy is to use papers that are natural, renewable and recyclable products and made from wood grown in sustainable forests. The logging and manufacturing processes are expected to conform to the environmental regulations of the country of origin.

Orders: please contact Bookpoint Ltd, 130 Milton Park, Abingdon, Oxon OX14 4SB. Telephone: (44) 01235 827720. Fax: (44) 01235 400454. Lines are open 9.00–5.00, Monday to Saturday, with a 24-hour message answering service. Visit our website at www.hoddereducation.co.uk

© J A Cloake, L Pellow, P M Johnson 2013
First published in 2013 by
Hodder Education,
An Hachette UK Company
338 Euston Road
London NW1 3BH

Impression number   3
Year   2018 2017 2016 2015

Cover photo © The Gallery Collection/Corbis

Illustrations by Datapage (India) Pvt. Ltd.

Typeset in 11/13 Frutiger LT Std by Integra Software Services Pvt. Ltd., Pondicherry, India.

Printed in Spain

A catalogue record for this title is available from the British Library

ISBN: 978 1471 831782

How to get the most from this book

This book will help you revise for:

- the Development Study (Medicine Through Time) and
- the Depth Study (either The American West, 1840–95 or Germany, 1919–45) for the AQA GCSE Schools History Project specification.

Use the revision planner on the next page to track your progress, topic by topic. Tick each box when you have:

1. revised and understood a topic
2. answered the exam practice questions
3. checked your answers online.

☑ **Tick to track your progress**

Key term

Key terms are highlighted the first time they appear, with an explanation nearby in the margin. As you work through this book highlight other key ideas and add your own notes. Make this **your** book.

Exam tip

Throughout the book there are exam tips that explain how you can boost your final grade.

Revision task / tip

Use these tasks / tips to make sure that you have understood every topic and to help you record the key information about each topic.

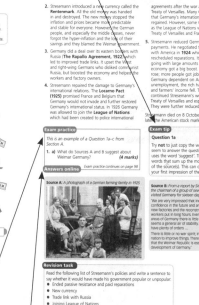

☑ **Tick to track your progress as you revise each element of the key content.**

Exam practice

Sample exam questions are provided for each topic. Use them to consolidate your revision and practise your exam skills.

Answers online

Go online to check your answers to the exam questions and try out the quick quizzes at **www.therevisionbutton. co.uk/myrevisionnotes**.

Contents and revision planner

Introduction: Revision and exam technique

Your brain is like a very tiny but extremely detailed filing system. When you go into an exam, the history section of it will be crammed full of content knowledge. You need to be able to retrieve this knowledge.

- **Revision technique** gets the knowledge into the filing cabinet in the first place.
- **Exam technique** helps you take out the right file and organise the knowledge into an answer.

Revision technique

When faced with revising for GCSE History, most students say:

HOW CAN I REMEMBER IT ALL ?

There are many different methods of revision. The key advice is to keep revising but only in small sections at a time. You have to be very organised to plan out revision sessions well in advance of the exam, and very disciplined to stick to your plan. The more you use the information, the better you will remember it.

Mnemonics

Mnemonics are an incredibly useful way of remembering linked items. You can either use the first letters of each item to make up a complete word, or you can use those letters to make up a new phrase which is easier to remember.

For example, say you need to remember the chronology of the History of Medicine:

What you need to remember ...	A much easier way to remember is ...
Prehistoric **E**gyptian **G**reece **R**ome **M**iddle Ages **R**enaissance **18th**, **19th** and **20th** **centuries**	**P**lease **E**at **G**reens **R**ather **M**ore **R**egularly, **18, 19** or **20** times a week!

You can make up your own mnemonics as you go through this book. Make them as silly as you want, draw little doodles – anything that will help you to remember.

Memory maps

Memory maps are a good way to remember a whole topic like the history of surgery, or a smaller topic like the story of penicillin. These are good because you can make links between bits of information, chronology or themes/topics by drawing branches or arrows. You can add your own colour, doodles and mnemonics to help your memory. It would be a good idea for you to build up these memory maps as you revise.

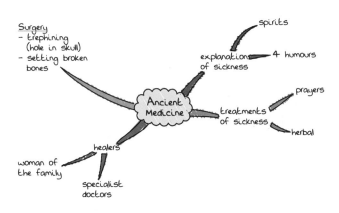

Key individual Revision cards

You need to remember the achievements of key people (these are found throughout the book). Make notes about these key people on a revision card, listing the following information:

- name and dates of birth and death
- area of expertise
- key ideas
- significance/achievement.

You could add any other information you think might be important regarding the key people in addition to the suggested points above.

Exam technique

This advice reflects the arrangements for the summer examination from 2015 onwards.

You will sit **two** exams at the end of your course. Both exams last for 1 hour and 45 minutes.

Paper 1: Study in Development: Medicine Through Time (40401A)

This tests your knowledge of the three themes: 'Disease and Infection' or 'Public Health' or 'Surgery and Anatomy'.

Section A
- This is compulsory and is on a different theme each year. You will need to revise all three themes to be ready for the exam.
- Questions in Section A are based on three images – Sources A, B and C.
- You **must** answer **all** the questions.
- Spend about 55 minutes on this section. It carries 30 marks.

Question 1a
- You need to use your knowledge to show you understand what is shown in a source.
- Begin your answer by saying **what** you can see happening, then go on to explain **how** and **why** it is happening.
- Always try to offer at least two points in your answer.

Question 1b
- This builds on Question 1a. It shows another image from a later period.
- Use the same 'what, how, why' approach as in Question 1a.
- You need to explain how Source B shows a different understanding from Source A.
- **'Whereas'** is a great word to join your ideas about the two sources.

Question 1c
- This builds on Questions 1a and b. You now have to give reasons **why** Sources A and B are different.

- To help you go through the **factor** checklist – **R**eligion, **I**ndividuals, **S**cience and Technology and **C**ommunications. Each of these might help explain the differences between Sources A and B.

Question 1d
- This will give you a factor to evaluate. For example, the role of *individuals* in the development of Public Health
- Source C will give you ideas about the factor. Your answer can use all of your knowledge of the subject. It is not limited to what the source shows.
- There are an extra 4 marks available for Spelling, Punctuation and Grammar (SPaG).

Sections B and C
Sections B and C cover the two themes that were not tested in Section A. You have to answer one question on each theme. However, unlike Section A, you have a choice of question, so **read all the questions** before you make your choice.

Each question will have two parts.
- Question **a** is as simple as it looks! You just have to show your knowledge of one bullet point.
- For Question **b** you have to compare **both** bullet points. You need to evaluate the contribution or impact of both theories, people, periods or developments.
- This table will help you plan your approach to Question **b**. We show you how to use it on page 35.

Introduction: *In both these …*	
Positive points about first bullet:	**Negative points about first bullet:**
Positive points about second bullet:	**Negative points about second bullet:**
Conclusion (your judgement supported by reasons from the lists above):	

You can see the question types in the table below. It also shows you where you can find practice and advice on each question type.

Development Study: Section A – Question 1				Medicine
a	What does Source A suggest about …?	4	*Source comprehension and knowledge*	13, 28, 30, 45
b	What different … is suggested by Source B?	6	*As Question 1a but add cross-reference*	45
c	Why was … different at these times?	8	*Explaining how factors have affected medicine (and SPaG)*	45
d	How important have … been in improving …?	8 (+4)		(51)
Development Study: Section B and C – Questions 2 to 5				
a	Choose one … below. What did …?	4	*Knowledge*	2, 26, 40
b	Which of … contributed more to …?	8	*Knowledge, understanding and evaluation*	21, 35, 40, 55

Paper 2: Study in Depth – American West (90402A) or Germany (90402D)

We have covered the two most popular depth studies in this book (The American West and Nazi Germany) but you only have to study one!

- The paper structure is quite similar to Paper 1.
- You can see the question types in the table below. They are quite similar to the questions in Paper 1.

Section A

- Section A has five compulsory source-based questions. Each question builds on the knowledge of the previous one based on sources (A–E).
- Spend about 60 minutes on Section A. It carries 36 marks.

Question 1a

- Source A will be a picture and Source B a short piece of text.
- Use your own words to summarise the impression the sources create.

Question 1b

- This introduces another picture (Source C) and another piece of text (Source D). Use the same approach that you used in Question 1a.
- Start with Sources C and D, then compare with Sources A and B.
- Use **'whereas'** to join your ideas about the way the **two sets** of sources are different.

Question 1c

- You must give reasons **why** there is a difference between the two sets of sources.

Question 1d

- Look at the content of the source. Say how it connects with what you have learned. Does it provide some useful insight?
- Then consider the ascription (caption), which explains where it has come from, because that will affect its usefulness.

Question 1e

- This question will test your understanding of why an event happened. You need to write about several reasons in detail.

Section B

- You will need to choose either Question 2 or Question 3. Each question has three parts. Make sure you read all the parts of both questions before you choose.
- Part **c** carries 12 marks (plus 4 for SPaG) so is a quarter of the overall mark. Think about how well you can answer the **c** part of each question before you make your choice.
- Spend about 45 minutes on Section B. It carries 24 marks.

Question a

- Part a is as simple as it looks! You just have to show your knowledge.

Question b

- Source F or G might be a picture or a piece of text.
- You need to use own knowledge and the source.
- You won't lose marks if you don't use the picture, but it will help with the answer.

Question c

- This question starts with a statement which is **an interpretation**.
- The statement takes a view on the issue or problem that you are being asked about.
- You have to write a balanced answer showing ways in which you agree/disagree with the interpretation and reach an overall judgement on it.
- We call this **an iceberg question** because the statement focuses on just one thing but in your answer you also have to write about the things that are not mentioned.

Paper 1 and Paper 2 Question practice and advice

This table summarises the types of questions you will face and the final column shows where you can find practice and advice.

	Depth Study: Section A – Question 1				American West	Germany
a	What do Sources A and B suggest …?	4	Source comprehension and knowledge		78	97
b	What different … is suggested by Sources C and D?	6			78	98
c	Why do you think Sources … give a different view …?	6	Source evaluation and knowledge		78	98
d	How useful is Source E for …?	8			83, 91	110
e	Why were … able to …?	10	Knowledge and explanation		66	108
	Depth Study: Section B – Questions 2 or 3					
a	Why was … important?	4	Source comprehension and knowledge			117
b	Using Source F/G … and your own knowledge explain…	8	Source comprehension and knowledge		72, 79	114, 115, 117
c	How far do you agree with this interpretation of …?	12 (+4)	The 'iceberg' question. Evaluation of an interpretation using knowledge and understanding (and SPaG)		59, 77, 89	103, 105

Medicine Through Time – The Big Picture

TIME PERIOD	PREHISTORY	EGYPT	GREECE	ROME
DATES	10,000BC–3000BC	3000BC–1500BC	1000BC–250BC	300BC–C.AD500
DISEASE + INFECTION WHAT caused disease?	Gods and spirits	Blocked channels (think of the Nile!)	Imbalance of the four humours Astrology/movement of the planets	
WHO healed it?	Medicine men, wise women	Specially trained priests Specialist doctors	Asclepius	
HOW did they treat it?	Herbal remedies, prayers and charms	Purging	Bleeding, purging, rest, exercise, diet	
SURGERY + ANATOMY WHAT, if any, surgery was performed?	Simple surgery – setting bones/trephining			Honey, wine and vinegar used as antiseptics Some simple anaesthetics made from plants
HOW MUCH did they know about the body and anatomy?	Very basic – knowledge of main bones and some organs			Galen thought dissection was important, but was only allowed to dissect animals. He therefore made a lot of discoveries that were not correct in relation to humans
PUBLIC HEALTH Was anything done to improve the health of the general population?	Individuals took care of themselves		The Greeks had some knowledge of hygiene but didn't understand why it helped you stay healthy	Romans built public health facilities – baths, toilets, sewers, aqueducts
WHO were the key people in each time period?		Imhotep	Hippocrates	Galen

MIDDLE AGES	RENAISSANCE	1800s	1900s – PRESENT DAY
AD1000–AD1400	AD1400–AD1600	1800–99	1900 – NOW
Miasma/bad air	A lot of people still believed in the theory of the four humours and that bad air caused disease.	Germ Theory: Scientific advances led to the correct understanding of … GERMS! Spontaneous generation	Genetic causes – DNA
A lot of people up until the end of the renaissance would rely on priests or family members to help them recover from an illness, rather than see a doctor or go to a hospital		Fully trained doctors and nurses, improved hospitals	
Leeches	More herbs available for herbal remedies	Vaccination discovered as a method for preventing disease	Chemical drugs, antibiotics, genetic medicine
Battlefield surgeons made minor improvements Use of cauterisation to stop bleeding	Improved treatment of gunshot wounds Use of ligatures to stop bleedings	Chloroform – effective anaesthetic Carbolic acid – effective antiseptic	Discovery of blood groups – transfusions
	Vesalius pioneered human dissection and proved a lot of Galen's theories wrong Harvey discovered how blood circulated through the body	Use of microscopes to develop detailed knowledge	X-rays Discovery of DNA
Monasteries developed their own public health systems after the Romans left, but kings and mayors did little to improve public health or fight disease		Governments became increasingly involved in improving public health Cholera epidemics forced the government to act	Help for poor, sick and unemployed NHS begins NHS – 1948
Al–Razi Ibn Sina	Vesalius Paré Harvey Paracelcus	Jenner Koch Simpson Lister Snow Blackwell Nightingale Anderson Chadwick Seacole Pasteur Hill	Booth and Rowntree Lloyd George McIndoe Beveridge and Bevan Fleming, Florey and Chain Crick and Watson Barnard

Factors and how they affect the history of medicine

Many questions in your exam will ask you about 'factors'. These are things that:

- **helped to cause change** – for example, the factor of **chance** allowed Paré to use his different method of treating gunshot wounds when he accidentally ran out of oil

- **helped to prevent change** – for example, the factor of **religion** hindered knowledge of anatomy as it banned dissection.

Complete the following table with examples mentioned in the rest of the medicine section.

Factor	Explanation of factor	Example helping change	Example hindering change	Page ref
Religion	Anything to do with gods or spirits. Organised religion becomes a real factor from the Egyptians onwards.	*In the Middle Ages it helped the development of medicine because there was a duty to care for the sick in Islam and Christianity.*		14
War	When countries are fighting each other, war causes and prevents change.	*Pasteur and Koch were French and German. They were making their findings during the Franco (France)–Prussian (German) war. This meant that they were competing all the time, both scientifically and for their country's honour.*		39
Government	The influence of laws and other rules on people's health.		*Governments did little to improve public health in the nineteenth century because of* laissez-faire *(non-intervention).*	50
Personal qualities	An individual and their story, where they made the effort or had the expertise to change things.	*Hippocrates was a brilliant thinker who came up with the theory of the four humours and the method of clinical observation. This improved medicine.*		29
Chance	Luck, something that happens by accident!	*Fleming didn't wash up his Petri dishes, and found penicillin living in them – which led to his understanding of penicillin as an antiseptic, which then led to Florey and Chain developing it as an antibiotic.*	In 1400BC Crete was devastated by volcanic eruptions which destroyed the public health system that they had built. The Romans had to solve problems that the Minoans had solved centuries earlier.	
Communication	This is about people communicating their ideas and sharing them so that they can build on each other's ideas.	*Any development during the Renaissance, when the printing press allowed books to be published widely and people like Paré, Vesalius and Harvey could spread their ideas quickly.*		18
Science and technology	Science is anything involving experiments or careful observation. Technology is the use of equipment.	*Science: Pasteur proved his germ theory using scientific methods.*	*Technology: Lack of scientific technology (microscopes) meant that people in the Middle Ages could never find out that germs caused the Black Death.*	

1 Medicine Through Time

Theme 1: Disease and infection

1.1 Medicine in the ancient world, c.10,000BC–c.AD500

> **Key content**
> - The treatment of disease in prehistoric societies
> - Natural and supernatural approaches to disease in Ancient Egypt
> - Ancient Greek Asclepian medicine
> - Ancient Greek Hippocratic medicine and the theory of the four humours

The treatment of disease in prehistoric societies

Revised ☐

How do we find out about prehistoric peoples?

- Prehistoric means before writing was invented. We know little about the lives of prehistoric peoples because of this. The evidence we have is from skeletons and burial sites, paintings and stone tools.
- We can study what the first people who could write, such as the Romans and Egyptians, said about prehistoric peoples.
- The prehistoric period ended at different times for different peoples. The Egyptians developed writing in about 3000BC. In Britain, the prehistoric period lasted until the Romans brought writing with them when they conquered in AD43.
- The Aborigine people of Australia did not develop writing until the nineteenth century. We can study them for clues to the lives of prehistoric people because they may be similar.

What can we work out from the evidence about prehistoric people?

- Most prehistoric people were hunters. They had to be nomadic as they hunted for food. The people were thinly spread out; an area the size of Britain would only contain a few thousand people. The hunters lived in small, isolated tribes or 'bands' of about 40 people.
- They lived in **temporary shelters or caves**. People moved on before much human waste had built up. This lifestyle was unlikely to pollute the water supply or attract disease-carrying insects.

> **Key term**
>
> **Nomadic** – always on the move, not settling in one place to live.

- There was **no government** and no one, outside the hunting band, to turn to if things went wrong.
- **Meat** was their main food and usually plentiful because there were so many wild animals and so few people. The meat of wild animals is usually very good quality. Prehistoric peoples made fires and cooked their meat. However, the cooking was not always successful and sometimes half-raw meat was eaten. People also gathered edible wild leaves, roots and berries. People probably knew a lot about different plants.
- Streams and rivers provided **clean water**. The nomadic hunting lifestyle provided lots of exercise for people. However, hunters could be wounded by animals or catch animal diseases (like anthrax or rabies).

Revision task

Make a table like the one below and find four things that might help prehistoric people avoid health problems and four things that might cause health problems.

Might avoid health problems	Might cause health problems

Prehistoric peoples had two sorts of medicine: natural and supernatural. These existed side by side. Both types of medicine were practised by the medicine man.

Natural remedies For illness they could understand, e.g. a broken limb	Supernatural remedies For illness they could not understand, e.g. a pain inside the head
<ul><li>These had been discovered by observation, and trial and error, and passed on by word of mouth from generation to generation.</li><li>Broken bones were set with mud and sticks for splints. Cuts were covered with moss or animal skins.</li><li>Natural herbs, plants, animal parts and minerals would be used to treat common ailments. Many of these would have proven medicinal properties.</li></ul>	<ul><li>It was believed these were diseases which happened when a person lost their own spirit or an evil spirit invaded their body. The medicine man's job was to restore the spirit that was lost or remove an evil one.</li><li>This was done by chants and dancing to contact the spirit world. The medicine man might drill into the skull (trephining) to release a bad spirit. Although this was a painful and dangerous operation with stone tools, we know that some patients survived.</li><li>To prevent it happening again the person might wear a charm which would often be the piece of bone removed from the skull.</li></ul>

Key terms

Natural medicine – treatments using substances from the world around them such as plants, minerals, etc. because the illness had a cause that could be explained by something in the natural world.

Supernatural medicine – treatments using prayers, chants and charms because the illness was believed to be caused by spirits or gods and did not have an explanation in the natural world.

Medicine man – a person who had knowledge of and power over the spirits. He used both natural and supernatural cures.

Trephining (or trepanning) – drilling a hole in a sick person's head to release an evil spirit.

Natural and supernatural approaches to disease in Ancient Egypt

Who were the Egyptians?

Around 10,000BC some prehistoric people began to stay in one place and farm – growing crops and keeping herds of animals. Farmers produced more food than hunters. When settled, sick people and the elderly could be looked after. Farmers lived a less dangerous life but the hard agricultural work affected their joints which gave them pain. Their animals could pollute their water supplies.

The Egyptians were one group of people who settled down in one place along the River Nile. The water from the Nile irrigated and fertilised their fields. They grew wheat, barley and flax which in turn allowed them to trade and become wealthy. They believed in gods and an afterlife which they hoped to enter when they died. They developed a written language called hieroglyphics.

How do we know about Egyptian medicine?

We know a lot more about Egyptian medicine than prehistoric medicine because there are many more sources of information:

- There are monuments and buildings with **inscriptions** that tell us about doctors and medicine.
- Eight medical books have survived written on **papyrus**.
- The bodies of wealthy Egyptians were preserved by **embalming** and were buried in tombs. Studies of the bodies reveal the typical medical problems the Egyptians suffered.
- Towards the end of the Ancient Egyptian period several **Greek writers** visited Egypt and described aspects of Egyptian life, including medicine.

Key terms

Papyrus (papyri) – paper-like sheets that the Egyptians wrote on.

Embalming – preserving the body for burial.

Ancient Egyptian medicine

Read the following statements (1–15) and then complete the revision task on page 10.

1. In Ancient Egypt there were many **full-time doctors**. Successful Egyptian doctors were well paid and the richest worked for the Pharaoh.

2. The Ancient Egyptians had an explanation of disease which was inspired by observing the fields that were irrigated by the **River Nile**. Their crops failed when the water did not reach them because the irrigation channels were blocked.

3. There were **female doctors** and healers.

4. Once a person had fallen sick they were treated with either **religious or practical remedies** or a mixture of both.

5. Some Egyptian doctors were **specialists** in specific parts of the body. There were, for example, dentists as well as eye doctors.

6. People thought they could avoid illness by pleasing the gods through prayers, sacrifices, chants and charms. They would **pray to particular gods** for particular illnesses. Gods protected different parts of the body, for example *Tawaret* was goddess of childbirth.

7. We know that **Ir-en-akhty** was a **royal doctor and the high priest**. A tomb inscription describes him as 'the king's eye doctor', 'doctor to the king's belly' and 'shepherd of the king's rectum'!

8. The Egyptians knew there were many channels in the body. They thought that the **body's channels (or *metu*) could become clogged up** with *wehedu*, which was harmful matter such as rotten food and faeces.

9. Many of the herbs and minerals had **medicinal properties**. Malachite used in eye make-up has an antibacterial action. Honey protects wounds from infection.

10. Doctors gained from being able to **write down their treatments** and see what had worked in the past.

11. Egyptians believed people could become sick if an **evil spirit** entered the body or if they displeased a god.

12. Illness could be treated or prevented by **unblocking the body's channels**. Egyptian doctors developed new treatments to unblock channels. These included making patients vomit or empty their bowels or letting blood.

13. One important group of priest-doctors worshipped the goddess **Sekhmet** in particular. She was feared as a powerful goddess who could send either sickness or cures depending on her mood.

14. Illness was treated by the use of **herbs, plants, minerals** and parts of animals' bodies. Most ingredients were local, such as honey, but some were obtained through trade with India and China.

15. One of the earliest known Egyptian doctors was called **Imhotep**, who lived about 2700BC. He was also an adviser to the Pharaoh. Many centuries after his death the Egyptians began to worship him as a god of healing.

Revision task

Statements 1–15 on pages 9–10 show that the Egyptians used a mixture of both **supernatural** and **natural** medicine. Some Egyptian treatments combined both types of medicine.

Make a large copy of the diagram on the right.

● Decide whether each statement is **supernatural, natural** or **a combination of both**.

● Write each statement summary (shown in the text in **orange**) in the correct part of the diagram.

● Use a different colour (or a different highlighter) for each statement depending on whether it is about:

— the causes of illness

— the treatments used

— who treated the sick.

Supernatural medicine

Natural medicine

Ancient Greek Asclepian medicine

Revised

The Ancient Greek civilisation developed around the city of Athens, and grew to dominate the Mediterranean world from 1000BC to 300BC.

1. Greece was able to build on the ideas of the Ancient Egyptians through access to their knowledge.

2. The Ancient Greeks are famous for their love of philosophy and development of new ideas based on rational thinking and belief. But they also believed in gods who could affect their lives.

3. Asclepius, the son of Apollo, was their chief god of healing. During the fifth century BC a religious cult developed that worshipped Asclepius and temples dedicated to him were built throughout Greece.

What happened at an Asclepion?

● Asclepius was believed to possess the **power to heal** patients if they visited his temples and made offerings.

● The patients believed that Asclepius was helped by his two daughters Hygeia and Panacea who would visit them in the **Abaton** and cure them. Asclepius was often said to be accompanied by a **snake** which would lick the affected part of the patient to help in the healing process.

● Patients came to an Asclepion hoping to be cured. Priests gave medicines.

● People could spend long periods at an Asclepion. The patients took regular exercise, bathed and ate a healthy diet.

● **Offerings and prayers** were made at the temple to ask for the help of Asclepius.

Revision tip

To help you remember the different aspects of early Greek medicine think of **A PRIEST**:
A **sclepius** – God
P **riests** – healed
R **est** – treatment
I **nscribed** – stones of thanks for cure
E **xercise** – treatment
S **nake** – visited
T **emple** – site

Key term

Asclepion (plural = Asclepia) – a temple dedicated to the god Asclepius. Some temples of Asclepius were simple; others were vast temple complexes with a bathhouse, gymnasium and a running track. The three most important were those at Pergamum, Epidaurus and on the island of Cos.

- When they were ready to be cured, patients had to sleep for the night in the **Abaton**. Here they were ordered to lie still with their eyes closed whatever happened.
- **Carved stones** were left by patients out of gratitude to the god to show that they believed Asclepius had cured them.
- **Asclepian medicine did not end when the new Hippocratic medicine started**. The Greeks respected their gods. Asclepian medicine was not painful or harmful and was free. Furthermore the new Hippocratic medicine did not always work!

↑ An Asclepion

Ancient Greek Hippocratic medicine and the theory of the four humours

Revised

Revised

Key person

Hippocrates

↑ Hippocrates

- Hippocrates was a Greek philosopher and doctor who lived from approximately 460BC to 377BC.
- Hippocrates changed the way doctors approached their work and thought about illness.
- Through his work and writings he has been called 'the father of medicine'.

The theory of the four humours

- Hippocrates gave his name to and led the way with a new rational and natural system of medicine. Hippocrates became famous for his **Hippocratic Collection** or corpus of books. The books carried his name but he did not write all of them. He wrote about the **four humours** and set out his theories about disease. The Hippocratic collection passed on his ideas to later generations and made them popular.
- This **theory of the four humours** was an important development in medical knowledge which was based on the work of Greek philosophers between 600–400BC like Thales, Anaximander, Pythagoras and Aristotle.
- They developed the idea that everything was made from four elements – air, water, fire and earth.
- This idea could be applied to the human body. In the human body these elements appeared as four liquids or humours that were **blood**, **phlegm**, **yellow bile** and **black bile**.
- Hippocrates and other Greek doctors argued that the balance of the four humours would be affected by the **seasons** and the actions of people; yellow bile in summer, black bile in autumn, phlegm in winter and blood in spring.
- The four humours needed to remain balanced for a person to be healthy; an imbalance caused illness.

- Later on in Roman times, **Claudius Galen** added his own **theory of opposites** which said that if a disease was caused by cold its treatment should involve the opposite – heat.

Clinical observation

- Hippocratic medicine put the doctor at the heart of the treatment of disease. **Hippocratic medicine** rejected the idea that gods, magic or spirits could cause or cure disease.
- To understand illness and the human body, Hippocrates believed that a doctor had to study his patient carefully. Hippocrates developed **clinical observation**. Clinical observation has four parts: Observation, Diagnosis, Prognosis, and Treatment.
- Hippocrates said doctors should observe and make notes about their patients, record their symptoms, consider and predict, and then base their treatments on knowledge gained from other cases and treat according to what was known to work for that illness.
- Using clinical observation the doctor tried to bring the four humours **back into balance**. For example, if someone had a fever they thought it was because they had too much blood in their body. The logical cure therefore was to 'bleed' the patient. Other treatments included laxatives and purging of patients to restore the balance of the humours.

However, Hippocratic medicine allowed diseases to run their natural course, with doctors giving treatments such as herbal remedies to ease pain. This was the idea of **minimum intervention** or doing the least needed to restore the health of the patient.

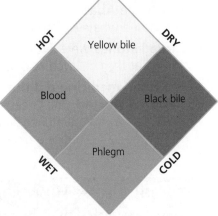
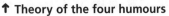

↑ **Theory of the four humours**

The Hippocratic Oath

Hippocrates created the **Hippocratic Oath**. Doctors promised to give their best treatment, not to harm the patient, and keep everything confidential.

Was Hippocratic medicine progress?

Yes

● The theory was a move away from supernatural explanations and towards natural ones. It was logical and seemed to make sense.
● It encouraged the close examination of patients for symptoms.
● The Christian Church backed the ancient writings. The medieval Church was a powerful organisation which controlled the universities and the training of doctors.
● Hippocratic medicine was followed by Galen who was the most influential doctor from about AD170.
● Claudius Galen was a famous Greek doctor working for the Roman Emperor from early AD160

(see page 28). He wrote 60 books explaining and adding to Hippocratic medicine.
● It lasted for 2000 years and was used to treat King Charles II in his final illness in 1685.

No

● Doctors in AD1400 still read Galen and followed the theory of the four humours in treatments. For hundreds of years no one dared say he was wrong.
● Some of the treatments such as bleeding could be dangerous and lead to infection.
● The theory stopped doctors looking for the real causes of illness.

Decide whether you think the following statements are based on **Hippocratic** or **Asclepian** medicine. Two of the statements are red herrings!

Statements	Hippocratic or Asclepian?
I was asked to pay for my treatment.	
I prayed for a cure.	
I had a nasty virus.	
I had to rest on a bench.	
I was bled.	
I was visited by the god who came in the middle of the night.	
It was free but I left a votive stone.	
It was because of my rare blood group.	
I was given a thorough examination.	
I was told that my illness is to be expected at this time of year.	

Source A: *A picture of Hippocrates with a patient*

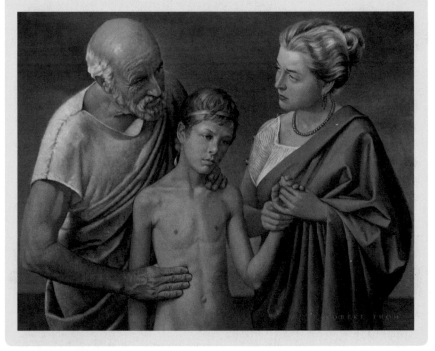

Exam practice

This is an example of a Question 1a from Section A.

1. What does Source A suggest about Ancient Greek medicine? **(4 marks)**

Answers online

Exam tip

For a question 1(a):

● always try to refer to what you can see in the source; study it closely

● question your first thoughts to explain them in some more detail

● always try to offer at least two points in your answer

● if possible make a reference to an earlier period of medicine than the one shown in the picture.

Revision task

Add notes to your own copy of the following diagram:

● to explain each part

● to say how it was or wasn't progress.

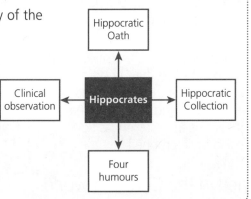

1.2 Medieval and Renaissance medicine, c.500–c.1700

When the Roman Empire collapsed, Europe split into warring tribes who had no interest in education or science. This might have led to the loss of all the Ancient Greek and Roman medical knowledge. This did not happen because Christianity and Islam preserved these medical writings. Muslim doctors and scholars added to the knowledge of the Ancient Greeks.

Key content

- Christian ideas about disease
- How Christians treated the sick
- The contribution of Christianity
- Islamic ideas about disease
- How Muslims treated the sick
- Islamic medicine's contribution to medical progress

Christian ideas about disease

Revised

People believed that illness was often a punishment from God, despite the fact that Hippocrates had suggested natural explanations. In the twelfth century Saint Bernard said, 'To buy drugs or consult with physicians doesn't fit with religion.' During the Black Death (1347–49) many people said God was punishing sinners. Mentally ill patients were thought to be possessed by demons and often flogged to drive out the evil spirits.

How Christians treated the sick

Revised

Despite these beliefs the Church had an important role to play in looking after sick people and this followed the example of Christ. In the early Middle Ages many priests and monks were also physicians.

The medieval Church set up several **hospitals**.
- Some were small, with space for twelve patients (a number taken from the Bible, i.e. Christ's disciples) but some were much larger.
- They did not have doctors but **chaplains**.

- It was common for monasteries and convents to have their own **infirmaries** for the care of the sick because it was their Christian duty. These infirmaries did not so much cure people as offer them care and rest. They believed God would make the sick better – prayer was the best medicine.
- However, many monasteries also had their own **herbalist and herb gardens** for the preparation of medicinal drugs.

The contribution of Christianity

Revised

- At this time the Church was the most powerful organisation in western Europe. It was very **traditional** and hostile to new ideas. For example, dissection to discover new knowledge was forbidden by the Pope.
- The Christian Church taught that important knowledge came from **ancient books** like those of Hippocrates or the Bible. Scholars worked to clarify what had already been discovered, rather than to discover new things.
- From 1200 doctors were trained in Church-approved universities where the works of **Galen** were particularly supported by the Christian Church. Galen wrote that God was the creator of the human body and that every part had a specific purpose. Anyone who suggested that Galen should be questioned or might have been mistaken, as Roger Bacon did in the thirteenth century, could be imprisoned.

Revision tip

To help you remember the different aspects of the Christian Church and medicine, think of **BUNCH**:

B ooks – preserved by the Church
U niversities – controlled by the Church where doctors trained
N o dissections – held back progress in knowledge
C are – for the sick as Christ did
H ospitals – built for treatment of the sick

The good things that happened in the Christian world

- They cared for the sick.
- They preserved the works of Hippocrates and Galen.

Islamic ideas about disease

The collapse of the Roman Empire led to chaos and war in Europe, but the Byzantine Empire in the East survived. Here, there was peace and stable government.

In the seventh century AD the Prophet Muhammad's followers established an enormous new, unified empire in the Arab world and North Africa. Islam's golden age of scholarship was from c.AD750 to 1050 when Islamic doctors made great contributions to medical knowledge.

Islamic doctors mainly followed the ideas of the Greeks and Romans, which they admired and translated into Arabic. However, some of them developed new ideas.

- Perhaps the most famous was **Ibn Sina** whose work led him to be called the 'Galen of Islam'.
- **Al-Razi** was also a famous doctor, who believed it was his duty to question the work of his teachers and thus progress knowledge of medicine.

> **Key person**
>
> ### Muhammad ibn Zakariya al-Razi or 'Rhazes' (c.AD860–925)
>
> - A Muslim doctor who wrote over 200 medical books.
> - In one of his books he identified the symptoms and development of smallpox.
> - He also wrote *Doubts about Galen*.

> **Key person**
>
> ### Ibn Sina or 'Avicenna' (c.AD980–1037)
>
> - Compiled a summary of all the medical knowledge that existed by the tenth century, called 'al-Qanun' or *The Canon of Medicine*.
> - This work included chapters on eating disorders, obesity and the medicinal uses of hundreds of drugs, making it more than simply a collection of other people's work.
> - *The Canon* was also used as a standard text in European schools and universities until the late Renaissance.

How Muslims treated the sick

Hospitals

The Islamic world had a very enlightened, even advanced, attitude to looking after the sick. Islamic doctors based their treatments on Greek and Roman ideas and methods (observation, the four humours, etc.) but also used improvements made by Islamic scholars like al-Razi.

- The first hospital in the Arab world was built in Baghdad in about AD805 and by the twelfth century almost every major town had its own hospital.
- These hospitals, unlike those in the Christian world of western Europe, were concerned as much with the treatment of patients as their care.
- More than this, there were teaching hospitals that stressed the education and training of doctors and nurses. One in Baghdad, for example, had its own library and medical school.
- Some hospitals in the Arab world were especially for people with mental illnesses and patients were treated with care and compassion.

Islamic medicine's contribution to medical progress

- **Doctors were supported in their search for knowledge by the government**. For several centuries the Islamic Empire was a single state ruled over by one man, the Caliph. Many caliphs were interested in science. During the reign of Caliph Harun al-Rashid (AD786–809), a centre for the translation of Greek manuscripts into Arabic was set up in Baghdad, the capital of the Islamic world. Hundreds of precious manuscripts, including the major works of Hippocrates and Galen, were preserved there. A library and study centre, known as The House of Wisdom, was founded also in Baghdad by Caliph al-Mamun in AD1004.

- **Muslims were encouraged by the Prophet Muhammad himself to 'seek learning even as far as China'**. In the area of medicine, the Prophet Muhammad also encouraged a scientific approach. He said, 'For every disease, Allah has given a cure', and physicians were encouraged to find those cures.

- **The works of Hippocrates and Galen were translated by Islamic scholars**, and added to by scholars like al-Razi and Ibn Sina.

- **Islamic medicine improved the drugs and medicine available**. Islamic 'alchemists' found new chemicals and scientific processes to produce them.

The good things that happened in the Islamic world

1. The preservation of the works of Hippocrates and Galen.

2. Treating the sick in hospitals.

3. The work of al-Razi and Ibn Sina adding to the established knowledge of Hippocrates and Galen.

4. The development of new drugs and medicines.

Revision task

Use what you have read about Christianity and Islam to draw your own version of the diagram below, to which you should add notes.

Islam		
Hindered medical progress		Helped medical progress
←		→
	Christianity	

Revision tip

To help you remember the different aspects of the Islamic medicine think of **B HARD**:

B aghdad – libraries of books of Hippocrates and Galen

H ospitals – for the sick

A vicenna – Ibn Sina, the author of *The Canon of Medicine*

R hazes – Muhammad ibn Zakariya al-Razi, famous doctor

D rugs – new ones developed by alchemists

Exam tip

It is common to get a question for 8 marks asking you to compare two periods, events, people or factors. You might be asked to compare and evaluate **Islam** and/ or **Christianity's** contributions to medical progress.

First you need to know what each did and then weigh up which contributed most to medical progress in the Middle Ages. Your knowledge here will help you answer a question about factors, for example comparing the impact of:

- **religion**

- **science and technology** or **individuals**.

Or it might help you tackle a question comparing the Middle Ages with another period, for example:

- **the Middle Ages**

- **the nineteenth century**.

1.3A: The battle against infectious disease since 1700

In 1800 people did not realise that germs caused disease. Some still believed in the four humours while others thought that bad air was the cause. Progress in successfully preventing and treating disease could not be made until it was proved that germs caused disease. After 1750 several key individuals made important discoveries in the battle against infectious disease.

Key content

- The discovery of vaccination to prevent disease
- Proof that germs cause animal disease
- Proof that germs cause human disease
- The discovery of how vaccination works
- How penicillin was developed as a treatment for disease

The discovery of vaccination to prevent disease

Revised

What was smallpox and how was it dealt with before Jenner?

Smallpox was a very infectious disease which killed 25 per cent of those who caught it. Those who survived could be scarred for life or left blind.

- People were often kept isolated and the disease left to take its course. You either died or survived!
- In the Middle Ages a way of preventing smallpox was used in China and India. This involved introducing pus, or scabs, from a person infected with smallpox to a healthy person. Giving a person a mild dose of a disease builds up resistance in the body and prevents them catching the full, killer form of the illness. This is called **'inoculation'**.
- Inoculation became more popular in Britain in 1718 when Lady Mary Wortley Montagu had her child inoculated. The doctors carrying out the inoculations could become very wealthy.
- Inoculation, however, was risky and some people caught smallpox and died from the inoculation. Nevertheless, the risks of inoculation were less than the risks of smallpox itself.

Jenner's discovery

Jenner had noticed that milkmaids who caught cowpox (a non-fatal disease) from their cows did not catch smallpox. In 1796 he took pus from a cowpox scab on a girl named Sarah Nelmes and placed it into two small cuts on the arm of an eight-year-old boy, James Phipps. Six weeks later he did the same with smallpox but Phipps showed no reaction. The cowpox had prevented him catching smallpox.

Key person

Edward Jenner

- Edward Jenner was a Gloucestershire doctor who, in 1796, discovered a way of preventing people from catching smallpox.
- He proved his theories using experiments and published the results, leading to greater acceptance of the idea of vaccination.
- He has often been called 'the father of immunology'.

Opposition to vaccination

Although vaccination against smallpox was a success, there was a lot of opposition to it.

- The doctors carrying out inoculation were against it because they would **lose money**.
- Religious groups said that smallpox was a **punishment from God** and it was wrong to interfere with God's plan.
- Many people **feared** that being vaccinated might turn them into cows.
- **Many doubted** that a country doctor like Jenner could have made such an important discovery. The Royal Society in London refused to publish his book on vaccination.
- Jenner was **not able to explain** how vaccination worked. It was another 80 years before Louis Pasteur would discover this, and then develop vaccines against anthrax and rabies.

Attitudes changed as people realised that vaccination was more effective and less dangerous than inoculation. Jenner also had powerful supporters, especially when members of the royal family were vaccinated. In 1853 the government made vaccination against smallpox compulsory for children.

Jenner as 'father of immunology'

At least two other people that we know of had used cowpox to prevent smallpox before Jenner. Jenner had such an impact because he proved his theories using scientific methods and experiments.

- His work on Phipps was carefully recorded and the results published.
- In 1799 he carried out a national survey which showed people who had suffered from cowpox did not catch smallpox.

Therefore, his idea spread in a way that it had not done before. Jenner may not have discovered the idea but he made other people notice it.

> **Revision task**
>
> This section contains a lot of information because there was so much progress in the battle against infectious disease after 1800. To help you make sense of it all, copy and fill in the table below as you read through the rest of this section.
>
> - Use one colour for those rows which are important for **discovering** knowledge about germs.
> - Use a different colour for those rows which are about **preventing** disease.
> - Use a third colour for those rows which are about **curing** disease.
>
> Refer back to page 6 for help with the Factors column of the table.
>
> | Key individual | Discovery | Date | Factors |
> |---|---|---|---|
> | Jenner | Vaccination against smallpox | 1796 | Scientific method |
> | Pasteur (1) | | | |
> | Koch | | | |
> | Pasteur (2) | | | |
> | Ehrlich | | | |
> | Fleming | | | |
> | Florey/Chain | | | |

Revised

Beliefs about the cause of disease before Pasteur

Although the theory of the four humours was less popular by 1800, many people still believed that sickness was a punishment from God or caused by miasma. The good news was that improvements to microscopes meant that scientists now knew that germs existed.

The bad news was that scientists had developed a theory called **'spontaneous generation'** to explain germs, which said that germs or bacteria were created when things rotted or decayed. Scientists had got it completely the wrong way around!

Key person

Louis Pasteur

- Louis Pasteur was a professor of chemistry at Lille University, France.
- He discovered that germs in the air caused an animal disease in silkworms, making the link between germs and animal disease.

Pasteur's discovery

In 1857 Louis Pasteur was asked by local wine growers to investigate why wine often became sour. Using a microscope, Pasteur discovered that it was germs that caused the wine to go off. Carrying out further experiments, Pasteur found that:

- germs made other liquids such as milk go sour
- this souring was caused by germs in the air
- these germs could be killed by heating the liquid – a process known as **'pasteurisation'**.

Broth is boiled

Broth remains free of micro-organisms

Curved neck is removed

Micro-organisms grow in broth

↑ **Pasteur's test of spontaneous generation**

Many doctors and scientists refused to believe his ideas so he designed an experiment with a **swan-necked flask** to prove that germs in the air caused decay. He carried this experiment out in public many times.

The next step was to show that germs could cause disease in animals and humans.

In 1865, while working for the silk industry, Pasteur proved that the disease which was killing silkworms was caused by germs. The link between germs and animal disease was made.

Achievements and limitations

- He had shown that germs caused an animal disease in silkworms.
- Many doctors and scientists accepted his ideas. In England, for example, the surgeon Joseph Lister was so impressed by Pasteur's idea that he began to use antiseptics to kill germs during his operations.

But:

- Despite his public experiments other doctors and scientists refused to believe his ideas and still clung to the theory of spontaneous generation.
- Pasteur had not been able to identify a germ that caused human disease. This was the final discovery needed to prove the germ theory of disease.
- In 1868 Pasteur was forced to give up his work temporarily when he suffered from a stroke.

Proof that germs cause human disease

Revised

How did Koch make his discovery?

- Between 1870 and 1871 France and Germany were at war. As a German, Koch was motivated by fierce **national rivalry** with the French scientist, Pasteur.
- He employed a highly **skilled team** of assistants and researchers to help him.
- Koch's methods made it **easier to study germs** by:
  - using new industrial dyes to stain individual germs so that they could be seen
  - devising a way to grow a group of the same germs
  - developing a way of photographing germs so that information could be shared.

Koch's achievements

Working after 1872 as a district medical officer in Germany, Koch made an important contribution to the battle against infectious disease.

- Using his new methods Koch was able to identify the germ that caused tuberculosis.
- Other scientists began using Koch's methods and soon the germs causing typhoid, diphtheria and pneumonia had been identified.

> **Key person**
>
> **Robert Koch**
>
> - Robert Koch was a German doctor who, in 1882, identified the specific germ that caused the human disease of tuberculosis. This was the final proof that germs caused human disease.
> - He was awarded the Nobel Prize in Physiology or Medicine in 1905 for his tuberculosis findings.
> - He is now considered one of the founders of bacteriology.

The discovery of how vaccination works

Revised

Louis Pasteur (again!)

In 1877 Pasteur was sufficiently recovered from his stroke to begin work again. He now discovered how vaccines worked. Various **factors** helped him:

- France had lost the 1870–71 **war** against Germany. Pasteur was determined to gain some prestige for France to make up for this defeat.
- He was driven by **personal rivalry** with Koch who had received many honours following his identification of the tuberculosis germ.
- Pasteur built up his own **team of skilled assistants and researchers** to help him.
- **Chance** played a big part in his next discovery about vaccination ...

An accidental discovery

Pasteur was trying to find a vaccine against chicken cholera by injecting chickens with germs but they always died. By accident one of Pasteur's assistants left some germs open to the air which weakened them. When the chickens were injected with these germs, they survived. More importantly these chickens also survived when they were then injected with fresh, strong germs. The weakened germs had protected the chickens from the strong germs.

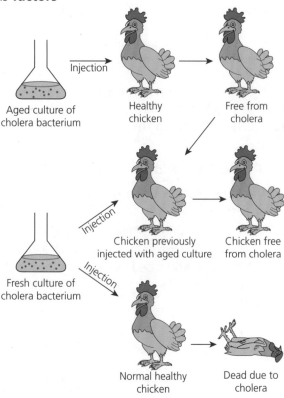

↑ **Pasteur's chicken cholera experiment**

More of Pasteur's achievements

- He had shown **how vaccination worked**. Injecting a weakened form of a disease built up the body's own defences so that it was able to fight off the strong version of the disease.
- Next Pasteur developed a vaccine against the deadly animal disease of **anthrax**. This saved the French farming industry a lot of money. In 1881 Pasteur successfully tested his anthrax vaccine in front of politicians, farmers and journalists and the results were quickly sent around Europe by electric telegraph.
- In the early 1880s Pasteur developed a vaccine for the deadly human disease of **rabies** but was reluctant to test it on a person in case they died. In 1885 a boy was brought to him who had just been bitten by a rabid dog. Pasteur gave him the rabies vaccine and he survived. Pasteur had now proved that vaccines worked on human, as well as animal, diseases.
- Other scientists used Pasteur's methods to develop vaccines for other diseases such as **diphtheria** and **tuberculosis**.

Important discoveries in the twentieth century

Thanks to the work of Jenner, Pasteur and Koch, the germ theory of disease had been accepted and ways of preventing disease by vaccination had been found. The next stage in the battle against infectious disease was to find cures for people who were already infected.

- In 1909 a German doctor, Paul Ehrlich, found a chemical cure (Salvarsan 606) for syphilis. Ehrlich described it as a **'magic bullet'** because it went straight to the harmful germ and destroyed it but without harming the rest of the body.
- Over the next twenty years other magic bullets were found but these were not effective against many germs. A new, more powerful 'magic bullet' was needed. This was to be **penicillin**.

How penicillin was developed as a treatment for disease

Revised ☐

The story of penicillin

Stage 1: 1928 – The discovery of penicillin by Alexander Fleming

- Alexander Fleming was a Scottish doctor and scientist who had seen firsthand how soldiers in the First World War died, not from their wounds but from simple infections caused by germs getting into those wounds. After the war he began to look for a 'magic bullet' that would kill those germs. (Factor involved – war)

- In 1928, while tidying up his laboratory, he made an accidental discovery. Fleming saw a mysterious mould growing in one of his old culture dishes that seemed to have killed all the harmful bacteria around it. (Factor involved – chance)

- Fleming realised the mould was worth investigating, and on examination found it was penicillin, the properties of which had been known about for over 100 years. (Factor involved – personal qualities)

- The mould had to be turned into a pure drug if penicillin was to be an effective 'magic bullet' against human disease. Fleming was unable to do this as he could not get the specialist help or money to carry on with his research. In 1929 he published his findings and did no more work on penicillin.

Stage 2: 1938–41 – Producing pure penicillin

- In the 1930s Howard Florey was leading a team of scientists working at Oxford University on how germs could be killed. One of the team, Ernst Chain, found Fleming's published paper while reviewing the research on antibiotic substances and Florey decided to see if they could produce and experiment with pure penicillin. (Factor involved – scientific method)

- By 1940 they had produced small amounts of penicillin which they successfully tested on mice. In October 1940 they tried it out for the first time on a human – a policeman suffering from blood poisoning. He began recovering but then died when supplies of penicillin ran out. (Factor involved – scientific method)

- The British government or large chemical companies might have provided the resources to mass-produce the drug, but both saw the war effort against Nazi Germany as a greater priority. (Factors involved – government, industry)

Stage 3: 1941–44 – The mass production of penicillin

- In 1941 Florey flew to America to ask the US government for research funds just as the Americans were about to enter the Second World War. (Factor involved – war)

- The potential of using penicillin to treat wounded soldiers and get them back to fighting fitness was immediately recognised by the American government. They gave $80 million for research and provided interest-free loans to companies manufacturing the expensive equipment necessary to produce penicillin. (Factor involved – government)

- The US government also demanded that the drug companies put aside their commercial, competitive instincts and share research data. Scientists from four drug companies were in constant communication as a result of improved rail transport and telecommunications. (Factors involved – communication, government, industry)

- Before long, companies were mass-producing penicillin and there was enough to use on the Allied casualties on D-Day in June 1944. Soon after the war, penicillin became available for civilian use and became known as an 'antibiotic', a drug made from bacteria to kill other bacteria. (Factor involved – industry)

1. Use the information on page 22 to make a spider diagram like the one on the right explaining the factors involved in the discovery of penicillin and its mass production.

2. When you have completed your diagram, use a different colour to draw lines linking factors that are closely related, such as 'government' and 'war' and write a note to explain the link.

3. Which one of the factors surrounding the diagram do you consider to be the most important? Explain why.

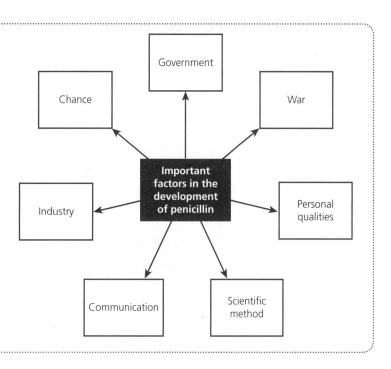

Make three sets of cards.

- Set 1 should have the name of a key individual in the battle against infectious disease on each card:

  - JENNER
  - PASTEUR
  - KOCH
  - EHRLICH
  - FLEMING
  - FLOREY/CHAIN

- Set 2 should have an important discovery in the battle against infectious disease on each card:

  - VACCINATION AGAINST SMALLPOX
  - GERMS MAKE LIQUIDS GO SOUR
  - GERMS CAUSE ANIMAL DISEASE
  - BACTERIOLOGY
  - GERMS CAUSING TUBERCULOSIS
  - MAGIC BULLETS
  - DISCOVERS PENICILLIN
  - PRODUCES PURE PENICILLIN
  - MASS PRODUCTION OF PENICILLIN

- Set 3 will have a factor on each card:

  - WAR
  - SCIENTIFIC METHOD
  - PERSONAL QUALITIES
  - COMMUNICATION
  - CHANCE
  - INDUSTRY
  - GOVERNMENT

You can use these cards in a variety of ways to help your revision:

1. Lay out Set 1 and place each card from Sets 2 and 3 next to the appropriate person. You could repeat the activity by laying out Set 2 and linking the cards from Sets 1 and 3 to each discovery.

2. Shuffle Set 1 and place them face down. Turn over the top card and try to remember the discovery and factors associated with that person. You could repeat this with the other sets or just shuffle and mix up all three sets together and try to remember the other information linked to that card. Add a competitive element by using the cards with someone else. Who can get the most cards by providing the correct information when they turn a card over?

3. You can make a set of revision cards by writing appropriate information about the discoveries made and factors involved on the back of each of the cards from Set 1.

1.3B The role of women in medicine since c.1700

Throughout history women had played an important part in medicine. There had been women doctors in the Ancient World and they had played a key role in everyday medicine as mothers and wise women with knowledge of traditional herbal remedies. Until the eighteenth century they had been able to qualify as surgeons and midwives. By the early 1800s, however, they had been largely shut out of medicine. Gradually after 1850 this was to change and women became accepted in the world of medicine.

Key content

- Why it became difficult for women to be involved in professional medicine
- How women became accepted in the world of medicine
- How nursing changed after 1860

Why it became difficult for women to be involved in professional medicine

Revised ☐

In the Middle Ages the Christian Church allowed only men to train as physicians. In the 1600s the Church did not give licences to practise medicine to women because it feared they might be witches.

- By the 1700s women could not go to university so they could not become surgeons.
- At the same time it became fashionable among wealthy families for male doctors trained to use forceps to replace midwives.

- In 1852 the government passed a Medical Registration Act. It required all doctors to belong to one of the Colleges of Physicians, Surgeons or Apothecaries. All were closed to women! Generally, it was difficult for women to gain a suitable education.
- There was widespread opposition in the male-dominated medical world to allowing women to qualify as doctors or surgeons. Society considered a woman's role was as a mother; any education she received was for that purpose.

How women became accepted in the world of medicine

Revised ☐

Despite all of these obstacles, two women (see below) fought back and changed the role of women in professional medicine:

Key person

Elizabeth Blackwell

- Although born in England, she had to go to America to qualify as a doctor.
- After qualifying in 1849 she returned to England.
- As she had qualified she had to be allowed to practise as a doctor. She was the only woman on the official list of doctors.
- She encouraged and inspired other women wanting to become doctors, including Elizabeth Garrett Anderson.

Key person

Elizabeth Garrett Anderson

- When she tried to train as a doctor, no university medical school would accept her because she was a woman.
- She was tutored privately and attended medical lectures at Middlesex Hospital where she worked as a nurse. She had to stop attending the lectures when male students objected.
- In 1865 she passed the Apothecaries (chemists) exam and received her licence to dispense medicines – the first woman in Britain to do so. The Apothecaries Society then forbade women from qualifying.
- She was still not able to work as a hospital doctor so was determined to gain a medical degree. She learned French and went to the University of Paris where she successfully gained her degree in 1869, although the British medical authorities would not accept this as it was from a French university.

In 1876 Parliament passed a law saying that women should not be stopped from gaining medical qualifications. The results of passing this law were that in 1881 there were 25 qualified women doctors on the Medical Register, and by 1901, this had risen to 212.

Revised

The situation in 1800

You will know from your study of surgery that hospitals in 1800 had a bad reputation (see section 1.6, page 36).

- Filthy, cramped and stuffy hospital wards with inadequate toilets encouraged infection to spread.
- Most of the nurses who worked in them were untrained. They were often criticised for being dirty or drunk.

As a result, anyone with enough money paid for nurses and doctors to visit them at home.

> **Revision tip**
>
> Women faced **bans** which stopped them from practising medicine. **BANS** gives you the initial letters of **B**lackwell, **A**nderson, **N**ightingale and **S**eacole – a handy way to remember their names.

Improvements in the 1860s

Through the late nineteenth century the situation steadily improved. The person who gets most credit for this improvement is Florence Nightingale. She improved basic hygiene at the military hospital during the Crimean War and saved lives. She then came home to a hero's welcome in Britain and used her fame to raise money and awareness and set up the first proper training course for nurses. Read her story in the key person box below.

> **Key person**
>
> ### Florence Nightingale
>
> - Florence Nightingale was born into a wealthy family in 1820. She trained as a nurse in Germany and returned to Britain to run a hospital for rich women in London.
> - In 1854 the Crimean War began with Britain and France fighting against Russia. Nightingale was asked by the war minister to take control of the main military hospital at Scutari.
> - She took 38 nurses with her and when they arrived in November 1854 they were all horrified at the squalid and unhygienic conditions they found there.
> - They thoroughly cleaned the hospital and even got part of a ward rebuilt. After six months the hospital's death rate had fallen from 40 per cent to 2 per cent.
>
> - When she returned to England in 1856 she set about improving hospitals and nursing care in Britain. In 1860, she set up the Nightingale Training School for nurses at St Thomas' Hospital in London with money that she had raised herself. Once the nurses were trained, they were sent to hospitals all over Britain where they introduced the ideas they had learned.
> - In 1860 Nightingale published *Notes on Nursing* which became a bestseller and she was consulted by hospital planners from all over the world.
> - Florence Nightingale became famous as 'the Lady with the Lamp' but not all women in medicine had such a long-lasting impact.

> **Key person**
>
> ### Mary Seacole
>
> - Born in Jamaica, Seacole became a skilled healer and midwife. She travelled widely, gaining knowledge of European medicine including how to deal with cholera and treat gunshot wounds.
> - In 1854 Seacole travelled to England and asked the War Office to send her to the Crimea as an army nurse. She was refused but paid for her own trip to the Crimea.
> - She set up the British Hotel near Balaclava to provide food and drinks for the soldiers. She also treated the
>
> sick and nursed the wounded on the battlefield, sometimes under fire.
> - Although Seacole's popularity and the respect that she gained from soldiers in the Crimea rivalled that of Florence Nightingale, her impact after the war was very different. After the war she returned to England with little money and in poor health. Attempts to raise money for her failed and nobody in Britain tried to use or learn from her medical skills.

1.3C Medical challenges and opportunities in the twenty-first century

Key content

- Medical challenges and opportunities in the twenty-first century

Medical challenges and opportunities in the twenty-first century

Life expectancy in much of the world has increased greatly in the last 200 years. However, there are still great challenges facing the medical world as well as exciting opportunities to make further progress.

● New diseases

A key example here is AIDS. According to some estimates it is the fourth biggest killer worldwide and, at present, there is no effective cure or vaccine.

● 'Superbugs'

These are bacteria such as the hospital infection MRSA. They are difficult to kill as they have become resistant to normal antibiotics. Thriving in hospitals and nursing homes, they lead to the deaths of thousands of people in the UK each year.

● 'Old' diseases returning

Although totals are small, the number of people in Britain catching diseases for which there are cures and vaccines (e.g. mumps, tuberculosis and malaria) is increasing. Sometimes it is because vaccination campaigns are no longer as effective, while in other cases the ease of foreign travel makes it easier for disease to cross national boundaries.

● DNA research

DNA and the genes it contains are the instructions that operate every cell in the body. The double helix shape of DNA was discovered by Francis Crick and James Watson in 1953. Between 1986 and 2001 the Human Genome Project identified the purpose of every gene in the body to produce a complete map of human DNA. Further research might lead to:

- ○ gene therapy where genes from healthy people are used to cure genetic diseases
- ○ genetic screening to see whether a person is likely to get a particular disease
- ○ customised drugs where drugs are created to deal with a specific gene in an individual person
- ○ the controversial area of genetic engineering where parents could 'design' aspects of their children's appearance or ability.

● The cost of medical progress and care

New drugs and medical technology are very expensive, while an ageing population means more money needs to be spent on social and medical care for this age group. The growth in age-related diseases such as Alzheimer's also poses particular problems.

● Illnesses caused by lifestyle choices

These give health services the dilemma of whether scarce resources should be used for people whose illnesses are caused by their decision to smoke, eat unhealthily, or abuse drugs or alcohol.

● International co-operation through the World Health Organisation (WHO)

This led to the eradication of smallpox by 1980. Amongst the many other programmes that it runs, the WHO is currently working to combat HIV/AIDS, malaria and tuberculosis worldwide.

● Alternative therapies

For example, aromatherapy or homeopathy. These alternatives to drug-based scientific medicine have become increasingly popular with supporters claiming that they are more effective than conventional treatments, although this is often challenged by the medical establishment.

Revision task

In the text on this page find as many challenges and opportunities in modern medicine as you can. Copy and complete the table below.

Modern challenges in medicine	Modern opportunities in medicine

1.4 Surgery and anatomy in the ancient world, C.10,000BC–C.AD500

Surgery in prehistoric times was limited. We know that prehistoric peoples could set broken bones. This technique was probably discovered through trial and error. Trephining (or trepanning) was a surgical technique but it was based on a supernatural belief. Real progress in surgery came when what was found out about the body could be written down.

Key content

- Surgery and anatomy in Ancient Egypt
- Surgery and anatomy in Ancient Greece
- Surgery and anatomy in Ancient Rome

Surgery and anatomy in Ancient Egypt

Revised ☐

What did the Ancient Egyptians know about anatomy?

- Although the Ancient Egyptian doctors knew about many of the body's **internal organs** such as the heart, the brain, the lungs and the liver they did not know precisely what these organs did. The Ancient Egyptian doctors knew the location of, and were able to recognise, the heart but did not know that the heart pumps blood around the body.
- The Egyptians also had an idea about the arteries and veins in the body although they called these '**channels**' and likened them to the irrigation ditches that flowed from the River Nile to their fields, watering their crops.

What surgery was carried out in Ancient Egypt?

- We know that doctors in Ancient Egypt could perform relatively **simple surgery**, such as removing growths or swellings on the outside of the body, sewing up wounds and treating broken limbs.
- Egyptian doctors were also able to **trephine** or trepan the skull, similar to prehistoric people.
- The Ancient Egyptian doctors had strong and sharp **surgical instruments** made out of bronze, as a result of improved metalwork skills at the time.

Where did anatomical knowledge come from?

- **Doctors** learned when they treated broken limbs, possibly of injured workers, slaves or soldiers.
- Information about the body's structure came from the **embalmers** who for religious reasons removed and preserved a dead person's internal organs because they believed that they would need them in the afterlife.
- **Priests** learned from the sacrifice of animals.

Exam tip

Be careful what you say about embalming leading to anatomical knowledge. We cannot be sure about the exact source of the Ancient Egyptians' knowledge because at various times the embalmers were regarded as unclean and were outcast from the rest of society. At other times some embalmers were doctors, so although it seems *likely* that the embalmers increased the knowledge of anatomy, we cannot be certain. Embalming is often used as an example of **religion** providing knowledge **but** also limiting it because the Egyptians could not cut up the internal organs to study them – they needed to remain intact for the afterlife.

Surgery and anatomy in Ancient Greece

Revised

What surgery was carried out in Ancient Greece?

Greek doctors were more interested in the causes of disease and sickness, and in treatments based on Hippocrates' theory of the four humours. But they did perform some surgical operations. In addition to setting broken bones, for example, Greek doctors knew how to treat pneumonia by draining the patient's lungs.

What did Ancient Greek doctors know?

In about 330BC Alexander the Great conquered Egypt and named the capital city after himself.

- At Alexandria the Greeks built **a university and a library** where books from Mesopotamia, China and India were collected, including works by Hippocrates and other Greeks such as Aristotle.

- Gradually this university and library developed into a **medical school** where dissection of human corpses was allowed (this was banned in the rest of Greece on religious grounds).

These dissections led to several important discoveries. For example:

- In about 300BC **Herophilus** discovered that the brain controlled the movements of the body rather than the heart (as was previously thought).

- Later, **Erasistratus** dissected human brains and developed this idea, saying that the brain sends messages to the body through the nerves.

Source A: *A set of surgical instruments dating from Ancient Greece*

Exam practice

This is an example of a Question 1a from Section A.

1. What does Source A suggest about surgical knowledge at this time?   **(4 marks)**

Answers online

- Erasistratus also dissected human hearts, wrote about the distinction between the arteries and the veins and speculated on the notion of the heart being a pump, an idea that would be proved in the late seventeenth century by **William Harvey** (see section 1.5, page 34).

Surgery and anatomy in Ancient Rome

Revised

The Romans did not make many new contributions to the understanding or the treatment of disease, largely borrowing ideas from the Greeks. However, they were important in providing public health facilities (see section 1.7, pages 42–43) and in surgery and anatomy.

The work of **Claudius Galen** (see key person box on page 29) is very important as he argued that doctors should learn as much as possible about the body's workings and structure. He recommended that doctors should wherever possible dissect human

corpses. This was not always possible because human dissection was banned for religious reasons. So Galen said that doctors should dissect animals, particularly apes, as they most closely resemble humans.

What did Galen discover about anatomy?

Galen regularly performed public dissections of pigs and apes. At one dissection of a live pig, Galen demonstrated how different nerves controlled pain, movement and the vocal cords.

As a result of such dissections Galen made several important discoveries, including that the brain, and not the heart, controlled speech. However, the anatomies of apes, pigs and dogs are not the same as that of a human being. As a result Galen made several mistakes. He said:

- that the lower human jawbone is made up of two parts, which is true of apes but not of humans
- the human kidneys were arranged one on top of the other, as in dogs, but again he was wrong
- the heart works like a machine, consuming blood as its fuel
- the body's blood supply can be replenished by eating red meat and drinking red wine.

These and other mistakes went uncorrected until Andreas Vesalius and William Harvey proved them wrong in the fifteenth and sixteenth centuries (see section 1.5, pages 33–34).

The impact of Galen

1. Altogether Galen wrote several hundred medical **books**, providing a comprehensive, coherent and detailed coverage of medicine. These books included the work of earlier doctors such as Hippocrates and contained Galen's own ideas on diagnosis, treatments, surgery and anatomy. Taken as a whole, Galen's books seemed **a complete encyclopedia of medical knowledge** and this was one reason why Galen became the supreme authority on medical matters for centuries.

2. Galen's ideas also fitted in neatly with those of the Christian Church and this was a second and possibly more powerful reason for Galen's work being unchallenged for almost 1500 years. During the Middle Ages, the Christian Church largely controlled education in Europe and, although Galen was not a Christian, he did believe that the human body was a work of perfection, designed and created by one god. **Galen's work agreed with the Christian idea** that human beings were created by God and, therefore, to question or challenge Galen was considered blasphemous.

Key person

Claudius Galen

- Galen was born in Pergamum, Greece in AD129. He studied medicine from the age of sixteen and even studied at the Greek Medical School in Alexandria.

- Galen took as his starting point the Hippocratic ideas of clinical observation and the theory of the four humours but extended these to include his own **theory of opposites**. This said that the balance of the humours could be restored by prescribing an opposite, such as a cold food like cucumber for a fever, or hot foods such as pepper for a cold.

- Galen moved to Rome where he gave public demonstrations of animal dissections. He established such a reputation that he was invited to become personal physician to Emperor Marcus Aurelius.

- Galen wrote over 350 books on medicine. Because of his reputation these books became the standard and unchallenged reference works for doctors until the Renaissance (c.1450–1650).

- So for at least 1500 years Galen was neither criticised nor challenged. The opinion of most doctors was that Galen could not be wrong.

Revision tasks

1. **Assess Galen's achievements**. Design and complete your own **Galen the Great** evaluation table similar to the one below.

	Galen the Great	Galen the not so Great
Ideas about the causes of disease		
Ideas about the treatment of disease		
Ideas and knowledge about surgery/anatomy		
Influence/impact		

2. Based on the information in your table, what would you conclude about Galen: was he 'Galen the Great' or 'Galen the not so Great'?

Revision tasks

1. Complete your own summary table for surgery and anatomy in the Ancient World, based on the table below.

	What surgical/anatomical knowledge did they have?	How did they get this knowledge?	Why did they not know more?
Egypt			
Greece			
Rome			

2. **Comparing knowledge of anatomy**. Produce a mind map to show how religion both helped and hindered the development of surgery and anatomy in the Ancient World. You could use green to show instances of religion promoting the study of surgery and anatomy and red to show examples of religion hindering the study of surgery and anatomy.

3. **Factor analysis**. Copy and complete a table like the one below to help you decide whether religion or individuals were more important in the development of surgical and anatomical knowledge in the Ancient World. Fill it out with examples from each period.

	Religion helping surgery/anatomy	Religion hindering surgery/anatomy	Individuals helping surgery/anatomy	Individuals hindering surgery/anatomy
Egypt				
Greece				
Rome				

Exam practice

This is an example of a Question 1a from Section A.

1. What does Source A suggest about the influence of Galen on medicine?   **(4 marks)**

Answers online

Source A: *A wall painting in an Italian church showing Galen (left) and Hippocrates. The painting dates from the 1200s, 900 years after Galen died*

1.5 Medieval and Renaissance surgery and anatomy, c.500–c.1700

Surgery in medieval times had not developed much since the times of the Greeks and the Romans. Surgeons were able to remove teeth, tumours (growths) on the skin, and to set broken bones. They also knew how to seal wounds by cauterising them, which meant closing up wounds by burning them with a hot iron. But the Renaissance brought with it a reassessment of past findings and developments in surgery through the work of three key people.

Key content

- Medieval surgical knowledge and techniques
- Renaissance surgery and anatomy
- The discoveries of Paré
- The discoveries of Vesalius
- The discoveries of Harvey

Medieval surgical knowledge and techniques
Revised

Medieval surgeons and their craft

- **Experience**: medieval surgeons learned from experience by watching other surgeons.
- **War**: in wartime surgeons learned how to deal with different battlefield wounds. They were confident in dealing with these kinds of injuries but they did not perform any complex, internal surgery.
- **Books**: the first European book on surgery was written by Roger of Salerno in the late twelfth century. In the fourteenth century Guy de Chauliac wrote a book called *Great Surgery*. These books contained hand-drawn illustrations of techniques such as cauterising.

Progress in surgery during the Middle Ages

- In the thirteenth century two Italian surgeons, Hugh of Lucca and his son Theodoric, found that **wine made a better job of cleaning wounds than water**. They didn't know how or why this worked; they just noticed that it did.
- In the fourteenth century John of Arderne experimented with **henbane and hemlock as anaesthetics**. In controlled doses this would have worked but there was always the risk of using too much and killing the patient.
- Some European universities had **professors of surgery**. This raised the status of medieval surgeons who physicians had looked down on until then. From 1340 an annual human dissection was performed at Montpellier University in France.

Renaissance surgery and anatomy

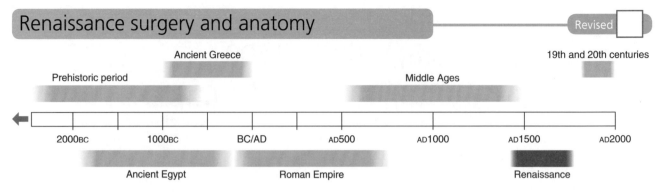

The Renaissance was a period of European history c.1450 to 1650. 'Renaissance' means 're-birth' and in that time many of the ideas of the Greeks and Romans were being reborn, or more accurately, rediscovered and reassessed. There were discoveries made in many areas – in science, the arts, geography and exploration, and medicine.

What happened during the Renaissance?

- The **classical knowledge** of Ancient Greece and Rome was rediscovered.
- They also redisovered the **attitude** of the Ancient World – enquiry. People were encouraged to look for themselves rather than simply accept what they were told. They had a **love of learning, experimenting and making new discoveries**.
- **The Church began to lose some of its power** over what people thought. People began to ask questions and, as we have already seen, some universities allowed dissection of human corpses without fear of punishment.
- **Printing developed**. In the Middle Ages books had been written and illustrated by hand. The printing press meant that identical books could be produced in their thousands. This led to the quicker communication of knowledge.
- There were **important developments in science and technology**: the workings of watches and pumps were improved.
- There were **developments in art**. Artists like Leonardo da Vinci were producing very detailed and lifelike drawings and paintings.
- **Humanist ideas developed** so that there was a new belief and interest in the potential and the achievements of mankind.

The careers of three men summarise the changes that occurred in surgery and anatomy at this time.

The discoveries of Paré

The situation before Paré

Before Paré surgery was often brutal. Open wounds and amputations were sealed by applying a red-hot cautery iron to the wound to seal it. Gunshots had boiling oil poured into them. This was very painful.

Paré's contribution to surgery

1. Paré used a new method of treating wounds using a **soothing ointment** made up of egg yolks, turpentine and rose oil. He began doing this when he ran out of his supply of hot oil to cauterise gunshot wounds.

2. He used silk threads, called **ligatures**, tied around the blood vessels to stop bleeding.

3. He also designed prosthetic (artificial) limbs for wounded soldiers.

The situation after Paré

Paré's methods, particularly the treatment of wounds, worked. His soothing ointment was far less painful than the cautery iron. However, Paré's impact and influence was limited in his own lifetime because:

1. **using ligatures was slow** and many battlefield surgeons felt they could work faster and so save more lives by cauterising wounds

2. ligatures themselves could cause problems; **if the silk thread was dirty it could introduce infection** into the wound and turpentine is not a powerful antiseptic

3. his **lack of formal education** meant Paré's work was looked down on by doctors and surgeons who had been to university

4. the **problems of pain and infection remained unsolved** for another 300 years.

The discoveries of Vesalius

Revised

The situation before Vesalius

Galen had been the unquestioned authority on surgery and anatomy for 1600 years. Doctors believed that Galen must have been right about the structure of the human body simply because his books had been around for so long. But some of Galen's knowledge was gained from the dissection of animals such as apes, pigs and dogs. As a result, Galen's mistaken conclusions about the human body went uncorrected for a long time.

Vesalius' contribution to surgery and anatomy

Vesalius produced the first comprehensive, fully illustrated anatomical **textbook**. He was influenced by the Renaissance spirit of enquiry and could dissect human corpses. Vesalius decided to repeat Galen's anatomical investigations. As a result he discovered several of Galen's mistakes.

1. The lower jawbone in a human has one part, not two. Galen had dissected apes and thought the jawbones would be the same in humans. He was wrong.

2. Galen said that human kidneys are located one above the other as they are in a dog. He was wrong.

The situation after Vesalius

Vesalius proved that Galen was wrong but once again his impact was limited. Why was this?

1. Many doctors simply refused to accept that Galen could be wrong. Instead they said that Vesalius must be mistaken, and arrogant for daring to criticise the master.

2. Secondly, Vesalius' work did not cure anyone and had no practical uses.

The discoveries of Harvey

Revised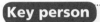

The situation before Harvey

Most of what was known about the heart and the blood came from Galen. Galen said that the heart was like a machine and that blood was its fuel. He also said blood was made in the liver and that people could help the regeneration of blood by eating meat and drinking red wine.

Harvey's contribution to surgery and anatomy

1. Harvey dissected animals and humans, performed careful experiments and kept detailed notes.

2. He proved that the heart pumps blood in one direction around the body.

3. Harvey showed that blood passes through the heart via the septum and that the arteries take blood away from the heart and the veins bring blood back to it.

The situation after Harvey

Like Paré and Vesalius, Harvey was correct in what he said, but his ideas had only a limited impact in his lifetime. This was because:

1. Once again doctors refused to believe that Galen could be mistaken.

2. Harvey's account of the circulation of the blood was incomplete as he could not explain **how** blood moved between the arteries and the veins through capillaries; this piece of information was missing until the development of the microscope in the later seventeenth century.

3. Like Vesalius, Harvey's work was of limited practical value at the time. It did not help doctors make people better until blood groups were discovered in 1901 and made blood transfusions a real possibility.

Key person

William Harvey (1578–1657)

↑ **William Harvey**

● Harvey was an Englishman who studied in Cambridge and Padua (in Italy).

● In England he was physician to King Charles II.

● Harvey was especially interested in how the blood circulates around the body.

Revision task

Create a table like the one below to show how the three Renaissance pioneers were helped by the features of the Renaissance.

	Ambroise Paré	Andreas Vesalius	William Harvey
The rediscovery of classical knowledge			
Enquiry and experimentation			
The decline in the influence of the Church			
The growth of printing			
Science and technology			
Developments in art			

You would be advised to spend about 20 minutes on the question below. In your answer to this type of question try to write about the advances made by the individuals listed. Balance up these points with some of the things that showed a lack of progress.

Paragraph 1 Introduction	Paré and Harvey were two great pioneers of surgery and anatomy in the 16th and 17th centuries. Paré was a very practical surgeon who worked for the French king. Harvey was more academic and worked in universities like Padua studying the human body. Paré worked in the 16th century.
Paragraph 2 Paré :)	Paré developed a new treatment for gunshot wounds. He ran out of cauterising oil and he observed other surgeons on the battlefield. The oil was meant to stop the poisoning effect of gunshot wounds. He used a soothing ointment to treat gunshots and his patients recovered with less pain.
Paré :)	Paré used a new method to stop bleeding. He used ligatures or silk threads to stop the bleeding rather than cauterising.
Paré :)	Paré wrote a book describing his techniques called 'Works on Surgery' in 1575. It was very popular and translated into many languages from the French.
Paragraph 3 Paré :(	However, Paré's patients still felt pain.
Paré :(	The ligatures could introduce infection to the wound.
Paré :(	Many surgeons preferred to operate at speed and ignored Paré's new techniques.
Paragraph 4 Harvey :)	Harvey worked in the 17th century. He discovered and proved that blood circulated round the body and disproved Galen's theory that it was used up by the body like fuel.
Harvey :)	Harvey proved this through observation, dissection and experimentation.
Harvey :)	Harvey wrote a book that explained his research and findings in 1628.
Paragraph 5 Harvey :(	However, Harvey could not prove how the blood got from the arteries to the veins because there were no microscopes powerful enough to see the capillaries.
Harvey :(	No one benefited from Harvey's discovery because they did not know about blood groups until 1901, and they needed this to do transfusions.
Harvey :(	It took over 50 years for Harvey's work to be accepted and taught to medical students in universities.
Paragraph 6 Conclusion	Paré made practical suggestions that helped patients. His work was done through chance, observation and trial and error. Harvey used a scientific approach; he was more of a Renaissance figure. Paré helped his patients and Harvey helped doctors. Harvey had a long-term impact and contributed to knowledge we use today whereas Paré's work was short-term and had defects in practice.

Exam practice

This is an example of the second part of the type of question from Section B or Section C.

1. Which of these individuals contributed most to the development of surgery and anatomy?

   ● Ambroise Paré
   ● William Harvey

   Explain your answer. Try to refer to **both** individuals in your answer. **(8 marks)**

Answers online

Exam practice

The question which follows is similar to the example on the left. Can you replace paragraphs 4 and 5 with similar points about Vesalius?

1. Which of these individuals contributed most to the development of surgery and anatomy?

   ● Ambroise Paré
   ● Andreas Vesalius

   Explain your answer. Try to refer to **both** individuals in your answer.

   (8 marks) (AQA 2011)

Answers online

1.6 Surgery in the industrial modern world, c.1700 to the present day

In 1800 there were no effective anaesthetics. Patients were sometimes given alcohol in the hope of reducing the **pain**, though most surgeons worked quickly. There was no attempt to control the spread of **infection** during or after surgery. Without any knowledge of germ theory, surgeons saw no need to clean their equipment, clothes or operating theatres. There was also no way to replace blood lost during surgery. **Bleeding** could lead to surgical shock and death. Therefore a patient who agreed to a surgical operation was more likely to die from the procedure than to survive. By 1920, however, this situation had changed and relatively safe, effective surgery could be practised.

Key content

- The problem of pain: Developments in anaesthetics
- The problem of infection: Developments in antiseptics
- The problem of bleeding: The discovery of blood groups in 1900
- Surgery in the twentieth century: War, science and technology
- Modern surgery: What problems remain?

The problem of pain: Developments in anaesthetics
Revised

- Surgeons could not carry out detailed internal surgery until they had an effective and safe anaesthetic.
- Operations had to be done as quickly as possible, and only on problems on the surface of the body, e.g. growths.
- In the eighteenth century scientific knowledge was increasing quickly. One scientist, Humphrey Davy, did experiments to discover the property of gases. He experimented by inhaling them. In this way he found that **nitrous oxide** was a natural painkiller. He called it 'laughing gas'. He said he could see it being used in surgical operations. Forty years later some surgeons used it successfully for the first time.
- Doctors now searched for other gases with similar qualities. The second gas to be tried was **ether**. Although this was successfully demonstrated in 1846 by John Warren in Boston, it was unpleasant, flammable and irritated patients' lungs.
- The breakthrough came in 1847 when the Scottish doctor James Simpson discovered the effectiveness of **chloroform**.

> **Key term**
>
> **Anaesthetic** – a substance that removes pain.

Opposition to anaesthetics

Not everyone believed that taking away the patient's pain during an operation was a good thing.

- Religious groups felt that **pain, particularly in childbirth, was sent by God** and should therefore be suffered.
- Doctors and dentists were **worried about the correct dose** of chloroform because they did not realise that men, women and children needed different quantities, and as a result some patients had died.
- Some doctors felt that anaesthetics **made little difference** to the outcome of an operation.

Much of the initial opposition to anaesthetics disappeared after Queen Victoria chose to give birth to her son in 1853 under anaesthetic.

The problem of infection: Developments in antiseptics

- In the early days following the development of anaesthetics, death rates actually increased because some surgeons now attempted longer and more complex operations.
- Surgeons continued to use dirty, unsterilised equipment and to operate in unhygienic conditions. Many patients died after surgery from infected wounds.
- Doctors and nurses saw no reason for cleanliness. There was no knowledge of germ theory and no attempt to keep hospitals clean.
- Until infection could be stopped, the development of anaesthetics was of little value.

Key term

Antiseptic – a substance that kills germs.

Ignaz Semmelweis

- Ignaz Semmelweis was the first to stop the spread of infection. He was a Hungarian doctor working in Vienna in the 1840s. He was horrified that so many women died after childbirth from puerperal fever.
- Semmelweis believed that doctors who had first examined corpses and then pregnant women were spreading the disease on their unwashed hands.
- He cut the death rate by ordering doctors to wash their hands in a solution of chloride of lime, an effective antiseptic which killed the bacteria.
- Although Semmelweis was correct, he could not prove it because Pasteur's germ theory was another twenty years in the future. His ideas were dropped when he left Vienna in 1848. Death rates rose again.

Joseph Lister and the breakthrough in antiseptics

- In 1867 the English doctor, Joseph Lister, showed that infection after surgery was caused by germs.
- He read about Pasteur's work on germ theory and developed the use of **carbolic acid** to kill germs. He soaked his instruments and dressings in it and used a carbolic acid spray to kill germs in the operating theatre.
- Lister cut the death rate in his Glasgow hospital from 46 per cent to 15 per cent in three years. With Lister's carbolic acid surgeons were able to perform safer surgery.
- His work revolutionised surgery by promoting the idea of sterile surgery to prevent infection.

Opposition to antiseptics

As with anaesthetics, there was some opposition to antiseptics.

- Some doctors thought the sign of a skilled surgeon was the speed with which he operated. Using antiseptics took **too much time**.
- Carbolic acid was **unpleasant to use**. Surgeons and nurses complained that carbolic dried out their skin and opened up painful cracks in their hands. Carbolic also made their eyes water and irritated the throat so that many actually refused to use it.
- Many surgeons still refused to accept Pasteur's germ theory and therefore thought antiseptics were **unnecessary**.

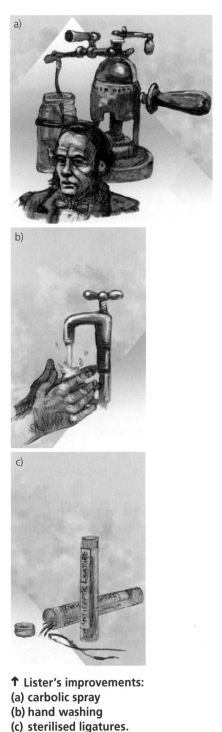

a)

b)

c)

↑ **Lister's improvements:**
(a) carbolic spray
(b) hand washing
(c) sterilised ligatures.

Beyond Lister: Aseptic surgery

Antiseptic surgery killed germs in the operating theatre whereas **aseptic** surgery was designed to stop them getting there in the first place.

> **Key term**
>
> **Aseptic** – a germ-free environment.

Developments in aseptics

- The problem of doctors and nurses refusing to use carbolic acid was overcome through the combined efforts of the German Professors Neuber and Ernst Bergman who insisted that all surgeons' clothes, hands and instruments were sterilised before use.

- The American William Halstead developed rubber gloves for all doctors and nurses to avoid contact with and the spread of germs. This removed germs from the operating theatre.

- By 1889 surgeons could operate without the risk of infection to their patients either by following Lister's use of carbolic acid as an antiseptic, or by using the new technique of aseptic surgery.

> **Revision task**
>
> These statements are about anaesthetics and antiseptics. Use two different colours to highlight those which are about anaesthetics and those about antiseptics. Add a sentence to explain your choice.
> - Surgeons could take their time with operations as patients no longer felt pain.
> - Surgeons and nurses were angry because of the extra work caused.
> - Many patients still died from infection.
> - Carbolic acid caused irritation to the skin, eyes and throat and could be very painful.
> - Pain was sent by God and therefore it was natural and good.
> - Longer and more complex operations could be performed.
> - Surgeons did not know exactly how much chloroform to give a patient.
> - Surgeons became ambitious and attempted more complex operations.
> - Deaths after the operation were reduced.
> - Infections among patients decreased.

The problem of bleeding: The discovery of blood groups in 1900

Revised

During surgery the body can lose a lot of blood, and patients can die from losing too much blood even if the surgery is successful.

- Blood transfusions were tried in the nineteenth century. They often failed because a patient's **body would reject blood from a different blood group**, and usually died from a reaction to it.

- Surgeons did not know about blood groups until 1901 when the German doctor, **Karl Landsteiner**, discovered them.

- This knowledge meant doctors could give **transfusions of a compatible blood group** to replace that which was lost from a wound or during an operation.

- However, there was **no method of storing blood**. The donor had to be in the same room as the patient. The replacement of a patient's blood could not be anticipated and prepared for; this came later with the use of **sodium citrate** to stop blood clotting.

> **Revision task**
>
> Make a nineteenth-century timeline like the one below. Place the events on the top or bottom of the timeline depending on whether you think the event was positive or negative in the development of surgery.
>
>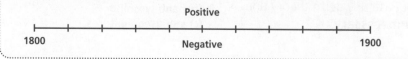

> **Exam tip**
>
> A question on surgery in Section B or C of the examination might ask you to compare developments in anaesthetics with those in antiseptics. The **Revision task** on the left will prepare you for such a question.

Conclusion

By 1920 surgeons were able to overcome the main problems they had faced in 1800.

- With effective anaesthetics they could **take time and care over operations**. They could also carry out procedures inside the body that had never been possible before.
- With the developments of antiseptics and asepsis, surgeons could **keep their patients safe from infection**, and so increase survival rates.
- With the development of blood transfusions, surgeons could **replace blood lost during surgery** and so complete more dangerous and complex procedures.

Surgery in the twentieth century: War, science and technology

Revised ☐

Many of the developments in surgery in the twentieth century were the result of **war** and developments in **science and technology**.

> **Revision task**
>
> Read the statements in the table below then try out the **Revision tasks** on page 40.

War	Science and technology
• During the First World War the demand for blood transfusions was huge. British doctors discovered that the chemical, sodium citrate, stopped blood from clotting and used it as a way to keep blood apart from the donor. • Gunshot wounds carried dirt deeply into the wound. War gave surgeons more practice at cutting away infected tissue. • The First World War helped develop X-rays as surgeons needed to locate bullets and shrapnel lodged deep within wounded soldiers. Governments ordered more of William Röntgen's X-ray machines to be produced and these, as well as more portable machines, were installed in military hospitals. • The development of penicillin during the Second World War (see section 1.3, pages 21–22) brought the decisive breakthrough in the fight against infection. • Plastic surgery and skin grafting was pioneered by New Zealand surgeon, Sir Harold Gillies. During the later stages of the First World War surgeons carried out more than 11,000 skin grafts. • During the Second World War, Gillies' cousin, Archibald McIndoe, used skin grafts to rebuild the faces and hands of RAF men who had been badly burned in plane crashes. • The conflict in Afghanistan that began in 2001 has produced many injuries that have led to new medical techniques to rebuild limbs shattered by explosions and advances in replacement limbs. • Wars are disruptive and cause governments to reassess their priorities. In wartime the priority is to save lives – 'crisis surgery' leads doctors to try out new ideas.	• German scientist, William Röntgen, discovered X-rays in 1895. Within months hospitals were using X-ray machines to see inside patients without cutting into them, examining broken bones and identifying infections. • While working in the late 1890s with such X-ray machines, the scientists Marie and Pierre Curie noticed that their hands were being burnt by the material they were handling. This was the beginning of modern cancer diagnosis, treatment and radiotherapy. • In the 1930s Helmuth Wesse pioneered the use of anaesthetics injected into veins. These helped recovery times and the success of the operation. Since then 'local' anaesthetics have been developed so that patients need not be asleep in some operations. • 'Tissue typing' was first used in 1962 to help match a kidney to a patient so that the risk of infection and later rejection was reduced. • Transplant surgery began with kidney transplants (1954) and liver transplants (1963). The first heart transplant was performed by Christiaan Barnard and his team in South Africa in 1967. • Micro-surgery was developed in the 1980s as a direct result of advances in technology. Surgeons today are able to reattach severed limbs and rejoin blood vessels and nerves so that use can be regained. • Keyhole surgery developed since the 1990s does not need large cuts in the body. Surgeons use a small 'keyhole' in the body to insert and use small tools, fibre-optic cables and cameras. • Successful transplant surgery is based on biochemical breakthroughs such as the development of drugs, e.g. cyclosporine in the 1980s to stop the body rejecting organs from a donor.

Revision tasks

1. Read all the statements about **war** and **science and technology** in the table on page 39. Choose three important developments from each category and summarise them in a table like this. (This table will help you with the **Exam practice** question that follows.)

	War	Science and technology
Before 1918		
1918–45		
After 1945		

2. Find examples of how the sciences (Physics, Chemistry and Biology) have influenced medical progress from the table on page 39. Record the examples in a table like this:

	War	Science and technology
Physics		
Chemistry		
Biology		

Exam practice

This is an example of a bullet-point-type question from Section B or C.

1. Which factor has contributed most to the development of surgery in the twentieth century:
   - war
   - science and technology?

   Explain your answer.   **(8 marks)** *(AQA 2012)*

Answers online

Exam tip

A question on surgery in Section B or Section C might ask you to compare two factors which were important in the development of surgery.

You might be asked to compare individuals like Simpson, Lister or Barnard, or you might be asked to compare periods such as the nineteenth and the twentieth centuries.

Modern surgery: What problems remain?

Revised

Surgeons are carrying out more complex operations with greater success but problems still remain. For example:

- Relatively little is still known about how the brain controls the functions of the body, so neurosurgery is still in its infancy.

- Transplant surgery has advanced to the point where a whole face can be replaced, although patients still struggle with finer motor movements such as speech and facial expression.

- Hospitals have seen the growth in infections and 'superbugs' such as MRSA over the last ten years. These are highly resistant to even the strongest antibiotics and more research is needed into their cause and treatment.

- Modern, high-tech surgery is very expensive and hospital trusts have to manage their resources carefully. They have to make difficult choices about who is in most need of an operation.

Exam practice

This is an example of a bullet-point-type question from either Section B or C.

Surgery

1. a) Choose one of the periods below:
   - The sixteenth and seventeenth centuries
   - The nineteenth century

   What were the main developments in surgery and anatomy in your chosen period?   **(4 marks)**

   b) Which of these periods was more important in the development of surgery and anatomy? Explain your answer.   **(8 marks)**

Answers online

1.7 Public health in the pre-industrial world, pre-c.1750

Governments provide public health facilities for their people in order to prevent them from catching diseases. Examples of public health are facilities for clean water, drainage and sewers, hospitals, and laws to prevent the spread of diseases.

Key content

- Public health in Ancient Egypt
- Public health in Ancient Greece
- Public health in Ancient Rome
- Public health in the Middle Ages
- The Black Death, 1347–49

Public health in Ancient Egypt   Revised ☐

- Keeping clean in Ancient Egypt was a matter for each person to arrange. The wealthy and the priests bathed several times each day using soaps and scented oils. Of course, it was harder for poor people.

- Egyptians wanted to be clean before worshipping their gods.

- When Herodotus visited Egypt in 5BC he was impressed with a code of hygiene that included bathing, shaving and the use of clean bronze plates and cups for eating and drinking.

- Archaeologists have found evidence of limestone bathtubs and latrines in the remains of the homes of rich Egyptians but the plumbing and waste disposal facilities seem to have been very simple.

- Some measures taken by the Egyptians were for comfort, fashion or beliefs but they 'accidentally' helped prevent disease. For example, Egyptians slept under mosquito nets to prevent bites which were uncomfortable. They wore eye make-up to look good without realising that the copper ore and malachite in the make-up prevented eye infections.

- For ordinary people hygiene was desirable but not always practical. Farmers and swineherds, for example, found it very difficult to keep clean and so were often shunned by the rest of Egyptian society.

Public health in Ancient Greece   Revised ☐

- Attitudes to health and hygiene in Ancient Greece were similar to those of the Ancient Egyptians; Hippocrates recommended keeping clean but governments did nothing to help people do this.

- Hippocrates advised the Greeks on 'A Programme for Health' as a means of keeping the four humours balanced. This programme, which became known as the **Greek Regimen**, recommended that both careful diet and regular exercise would lead to a healthy body and a healthy mind. Hippocrates recommended that the Greeks should eat more and drink less in winter, with meals of roasted meats. In the summer the Greeks were advised to drink more and eat less with a diet of fresh vegetables and boiled meats.

- The importance of regular exercise was emphasised in 'A Programme for Health'. Sport stadiums and gymnasiums were built all over Greece. The restored Asclepion at Epidaurus contains both facilities which recovering patients were encouraged to use.

- Sport, including running, boxing, wrestling, javelin and discus, was part of the school curriculum for Athenian boys aged six to fourteen. After exercise, showers were compulsory.

- Diocles of Carystus, an Athenian physician who had studied Hippocrates, recommended regular exercise such as walking, followed by bathing, then cleaning teeth.

- This way of life, however, was best suited to the rich who had time for exercise and bathing. Ordinary citizens, labourers, slaves, farmers and even craftsmen found it difficult to follow. Hippocrates himself realised this and suggested that such citizens should attempt to keep clean but that it was a matter of doing the best one could.

Public health in Ancient Rome

Although the Romans may not have made many contributions to the understanding or treatment of disease, they were the first people to plan and carry out a programme for public health, so that ordinary people and not just the rich could keep clean.

The Romans were very careful in choosing sites for their towns or settlements. They thought it was very important to build their settlements in places close to rivers and away from mosquito-infested swamps and marshes.

Features of the Roman public health system

- **Aqueducts** carried fresh water into the towns.

- **Water pipes** made from wood, lead or bronze brought filtered water into and around the town.

- **Drinking fountains** were provided in towns so that people could drink and collect water for washing.

- **Bathhouses** were built in even the smallest of towns. For a small fee people could exercise and bathe.

- **Latrines or toilets**, often seating up to twenty, were provided. These were flushed using water from the bathhouses which drained into the sewers.

- **Sewers** built of stone took the dirty and waste water away from the town.

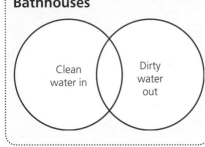

How did the Romans keep their army healthy?

The health of the soldiers in the Roman army was very important as the army defended the empire. Army camps and forts were built in healthy locations close to fast flowing water.

The army built military hospitals in England, Germany, Switzerland and Africa. In the hospitals, wounded soldiers were treated by *medici* or medical officers. Each hospital had its own sewage system and wards separated by corridors so that infections would not spread.

Why did the Romans provide such public health facilities for everyone?

- The Roman army had created an empire. The health of the army therefore kept the empire strong.
- The Romans recognised that healthy slaves, workers, merchants and traders were necessary to the maintenance of the empire.

Revision task

The Roman public health system ensured that clean water was coming into Rome and dirty water was being taken out of Rome.

Put these labels in the correct place ('Clean water in', 'Dirty water out', or the shared middle) on your copy of the Venn diagram below:

Water filters
Bronze pipes
Lead pipes
Aqueducts
Wooden pipes
Sewers
Latrines
Bathhouses

Clean water in

Dirty water out

- Roman governments were decisive enough to see public health as a priority and strong enough to see their plans carried through.
- The Romans had the engineering and construction skills necessary to plan, design and build the aqueducts, bathhouses, latrines and sewers.
- The Romans had a vast army of slaves who were used as labourers on the construction projects.
- Rome was wealthy. Taxation was used to fund public health projects.
- The people of Rome were proud of their city. Building public works demonstrated that pride, particularly when water was a precious resource.

How effective were Roman public health measures?

The elaborate and expensive public health facilities provided by the Romans may not have had much impact on the health of the people.

- In bathhouses water was usually only changed once a week and so was more likely to be a source of disease.
- In towns sewers were often open, or close to the surface. They also had a tendency to block so that bad smells were common, as was the threat of disease.
- The Romans were unable to stop epidemics and plagues. Indeed one such disease was named 'Galen's Plague' after he had researched its origins and symptoms in AD167.
- In villages there were neither bathhouses nor sewers. Away from towns, and the influence of government, collecting water and keeping clean was a matter for individuals.
- When the army returned to Rome in the fifth century, many of their towns throughout Europe were abandoned. Their public health facilities fell into disuse and then disrepair.

Revision task

The reasons for the Romans providing public health facilities for their people were either **motivational factors** or **enabling factors**.

- A motivational factor is a reason to do something.
- An enabling factor is the means to do it.

Sort the following factors into motivational and enabling factors and place them under the correct heading on the table.

Motivational factors	Enabling factors

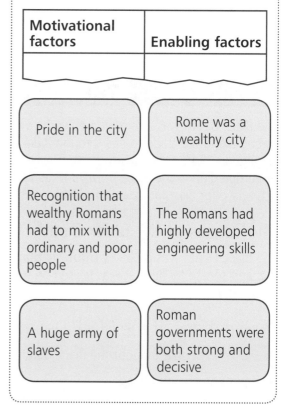

Pride in the city

Rome was a wealthy city

Recognition that wealthy Romans had to mix with ordinary and poor people

The Romans had highly developed engineering skills

A huge army of slaves

Roman governments were both strong and decisive

Public health in the Middle Ages

Revised

In about AD500 the Roman Empire was under attack from Barbarian tribes such as the Goths, Vandals and Huns. These tribes were illiterate and not interested in public health or engineering. As a result the Romans' public health facilities fell into disrepair and people's health came under serious threat.

In the absence of a strong government, medieval towns became filthy; waste lay about in the streets. The few public toilets or cesspits were often close to wells which provided drinking water or rivers used for washing and bathing.

Things only started to improve from 1200 onwards when, for example, cesspits were lined with stone to stop them leaking into water supplies.

Exam tip

Questions on public health in Section 2 or Section 3 of the examination might ask you to compare the effectiveness of public health measures in the Ancient World with those of the Middle Ages, nineteenth or twentieth centuries.

Why was public health so bad in the Middle Ages?

- People at the time had no knowledge of the need for public health and ways to prevent disease spreading.
- The Roman public health facilities had been destroyed or fallen into disrepair and there were no engineers with the knowledge needed to restore them.
- Towns were often full of animals such as pigs, sheep, chickens and stray dogs and cats.
- The unpaved streets were impossible to keep clean.
- Houses were tightly packed together.
- Paid officials found it hard to remove all the rubbish and filth.
- Governments were not strong enough to impose a hygiene regime on their citizens. Kings were more interested in defending the country and in keeping law and order than promoting public health.

Exam tip

Public health wasn't bad everywhere in the Middle Ages. In the monasteries, monks and the patients in their infirmaries had access to fresh water for drinking and bathing. Monasteries like Fountains Abbey were built on the banks of rivers.

The Black Death, 1347–49

Revised

The Black Death was a terrifying epidemic which began in China. It spread along the trade routes through India and Europe and reached England in 1348. Estimates suggest at least one-third of the population of Europe died in the years from 1347 to 1350. The Black Death killed rich and poor alike, quickly and painfully.

The causes of the Black Death

The Black Death was probably **bubonic plague** which was carried by rats and spread by fleas. It was passed on when infected fleas bit other rats or humans.

Explanations of the Black Death

At the time, people thought the Black Death was:

- a punishment from God
- the result of the planets being out of alignment
- the work of Jews, or other outsiders, poisoning local people
- caused by bad air, dead bodies or stagnant water.

Treatments for the Black Death

- Some people prayed in the hope that God would spare them.
- A group called the **flagellants** whipped themselves to demonstrate repentance of their sins to God.
- John of Burgundy, in 1365, advised people to avoid baths as opening the pores of the skin allowed disease into the body.
- He also suggested following Galen's theory of opposites, treating the fevers with cold foods such as cucumber and avoiding hot foods such as peppers and garlic.
- In 1349 King Edward III ordered the Mayor of London to remove waste and filth lying in the streets.

This is an example of a Question 1 from Section A.

1. a) Study Source A. What does it suggest about public health in Ancient Rome? **(4 marks)**

    b) What different impression of public health is suggested by Source B? **(6 marks)**

    c) Why was public health different at these times? **(8 marks)**

(AQA 2009)

Answers online

Source A: *The Roman baths complex at Bath built from AD70*

Source B: *The Black Death in Florence, 1348*

Revision tasks

1. Based on the information on pages 42–44 and your own notes, do you think people were healthiest in Roman times or during the Middle Ages?

2. To help you compare public health provision across time periods, make a table like the one below and complete it with brief notes.

Factor	Roman towns	A medieval town	A medieval monastery
Beliefs and values			
Wealth			
Skills and technology			
Government			
War			

1.8 Public health after the Industrial Revolution, c.1750–c.1900

The Industrial Revolution in Britain caused some of the worst public health problems ever seen in towns and cities. Towns grew dramatically as people moved in large numbers from the countryside to find work. These newly developed towns were not equipped to cope with such migration. The government, although reluctant to do anything at first, was forced to respond for a number of reasons.

Conditions in nineteenth-century towns   Revised

Living conditions in nineteenth-century towns were very poor. The Industrial Revolution caused towns to grow rapidly between 1750 and 1850 but there were no laws regulating construction, sanitation or hygiene standards.

- **Unscrupulous landowners and businessmen** built cheap, low quality, back-to-back slum houses.
- There were **no laws** forcing local councils to provide sewers, toilets or clean water. People got their water from **shared standpipes** in the streets.
- **Rubbish, human waste and animal waste** were allowed to pile up in the streets.
- **Stray animals** wandered freely and some people kept cattle or pigs in their homes.
- Existing sewers quickly became blocked, **water became contaminated** and foul smells lingered in the streets.
- **Disease spread rapidly** in these overcrowded conditions so that the quality of life and life expectancy were much lower in towns than in the countryside.

Revision task

Look closely at the following picture. Annotate the picture with all the things you can see that contributed to poor public health in nineteenth-century towns.

Cholera

In the early nineteenth century **cholera** was a new and deadly disease that killed its victims painfully and quickly. Cholera is spread by infected water. It seems to have originated in India and spread through the trade routes, reaching Britain in 1831. The cholera epidemic of 1831–32 shocked and terrified people who had never seen anything like it before. Because of this, people began to examine the victims' living conditions.

- **Boards of Health** were set up in some towns to try to prevent the disease spreading, though these were not compulsory. Most were disbanded when the epidemic died down.

- In 1838 Doctors Arnott, Kay and Smith **researched living conditions among poor people** in London and were horrified by what they found. Their study prompted a former Poor Law Commissioner, Edwin Chadwick, to carry out a nationwide survey of the poor and their health.

- Further cholera epidemics were recorded in 1848 and 1854. These made the wealthy realise that they **could neither ignore nor dismiss** the causes or effects of this disease.

- At the time there was **very little understanding of the causes of disease**. Some believed God was punishing sinners while others thought it was spread through the air (**miasma**) or by touch (contagion).

> **Key term**
>
> **Cholera** – deadly water-borne disease causing death through diarrhoea and dehydration.

> **Key term**
>
> **Miasma** – the belief that disease was caused by bad or poisoned air.

Dr John Snow

> **Key person**
>
> **Dr John Snow**
>
> - John Snow was a London doctor. He was one of the first doctors to use chloroform and ether as anaesthetics, and successfully used chloroform on Queen Victoria when she gave birth to two of her nine children.
> - He also came to believe that cholera was caused not by poison in the air, but by drinking water that was contaminated by the excrement of cholera victims.
> - He is often called one of the fathers of modern **epidemiology**.

In 1854 Snow mapped where the cholera victims lived and saw that cases were clustered around a water pump in Broad Street, Soho, where over 500 people died in ten days. Snow persuaded the local council to remove the handle on the water pump to stop people from using it. As a result, the death rate dropped dramatically. It was later discovered that a cesspool, less than one metre away from the pump, was leaking into the water and contaminating it.

Although Snow had seemingly proved the link between dirty water and cholera, many refused to accept his findings because they did not know why there was a link (remember Pasteur had not yet published his germ theory, see section 1.3, pages 19–21). Consequently many scientists and doctors held onto theories like miasma and **spontaneous generation**.

> **Key term**
>
> **Epidemiology** – the study of disease and populations.

> **Key term**
>
> **Spontaneous generation** – the theory that decaying matter turns into germs.

Edwin Chadwick

In 1842 Chadwick published his 'Report on the Sanitary Conditions of the Labouring Population', proving that poor people in towns lived in overcrowded and unhygienic conditions. This resulted in:

- illness and low life expectancy
- absence from work causing the sufferer to become poorer still
- those in work having to pay higher taxes to support the poor.

Chadwick's solution was for the government to provide public health facilities such as clean water, drains and sewers, clean streets, and to appoint Medical Officers to ensure these measures were carried out. He argued that towns should borrow money to provide such facilities and recover their costs through higher rates over the next 30 years.

While Chadwick's recommendations did form the basis of the 1848 Public Health Act, it took the government six years to pass the Act because of strong opposition.

Why was there opposition to Chadwick and public health reform?

- Many rich taxpayers objected to paying for improvements to facilities they would not use.
- Local councils resented orders from central government.
- Many people in government believed in the idea of *laissez-faire* (non-intervention) government.

Nevertheless, these objections were silenced when cholera started to spread across Europe again in 1847. In 1848 a Public Health Act was passed. It was the first of its kind.

> **Key person**
>
> **Edwin Chadwick**
> - Edwin Chadwick was a barrister and social reformer.
> - He was concerned about the health of poor people because he thought that disease and ill health cost the nation and ratepayers a lot of money.
> - He thought the best way of reducing the cost of looking after the poor was to improve their health.
> - Chadwick became the first president of the Association of Public Sanitary Inspectors in 1884, which is now the Chartered Institute of Environmental Health.

> **Key term**
>
> ***Laissez-faire*** – the idea that governments should not pass laws which interfere in the lives of the people.

The 1848 Public Health Act and public health reforms

Revised

Some of the effects of the 1848 Public Health Act were:

- the setting up a **National Board of Health**
- to give local councils the powers to improve the water supply and the sewers if they wanted to and had the support of their ratepayers
- to allow councils to appoint **Medical Officers of Health** as well as **local Boards of Health** to supervise public health improvements.

However, the 1848 Act was not compulsory. It suggested improvements but did not force local councils to carry them out. Some councils set up local Boards of Health; most chose not to. When the threat of cholera faded the National Board of Health was abolished in 1854.

The work of William Farr

In the early nineteenth century the government wanted to compile accurate information about its citizens and appointed an official, William Farr, to record data about the population. From 1837 all births, marriages and deaths had to be recorded by law.

- William Farr used these statistics to map areas with high death rates and looked at the causes of death. Like Chadwick he became convinced of the links between poverty, dirt and poor health.
- Farr's work proved that unhealthy living conditions and high death rates were related. His work shamed some local councils into action.

Joseph Bazalgette and the 'Great Stink' of 1858

- During the summer of 1858 conditions in London were especially bad. **The level of water in the River Thames dropped dramatically and the smell from the river became known as the 'Great Stink'**. It particularly disturbed MPs because the Houses of Parliament are on the riverbank. They realised the 1848 Act had not gone far enough and more improvements were needed.

- **Bazalgette was the engineer who designed and supervised the building of a new sewer system** after the 'Great Stink'. This incorporated more than 1000 miles of sewers, built with new materials like Portland cement.

- Instead of using the usual circular design Bazalgette designed the sewers as an oval tunnel. **This innovative engineering design made the sewers self-cleaning**.

- Bazalgette meticulously mapped the flow and the tides of the River Thames and connected his sewers so **the tides carried the waste away**. He **also connected the sewers to pumping stations** so that the sewage could be carried out to sea at high tide.

This was an ambitious project that took more than ten years to complete. Bazalgette planned ahead and anticipated that, with the steady rate of population increase, his system needed a higher capacity than was required in the 1860s. Bazalgette's original design and construction is still part of London's sewage system today.

Octavia Hill

Hill pushed for fair rent and access to open spaces for poor tenants, and campaigned against building on existing woodlands, including Hampstead Heath. In 1865 she started to buy slum houses and make them into healthy homes as an example of what could be done for working people. This concept led to the Artisans' Dwelling Act (1875) which empowered local councils to clear away slums for public health reasons.

Key person

Octavia Hill

- Octavia Hill was a social reformer.

- She put pressure on governments to make changes to public health provision, especially housing.

- As a teacher of poor children, Hill had seen for herself some of their appalling living conditions, and her family was also committed to social reform.

- Hill was one of the founders of the National Trust and believed everybody should have access to open spaces.

Revision tip

You should have been making revision cards summarising the achievements of key individuals. If you have not then it's not too late to start. On one side put the person's name and period. On the other side make brief notes on:

- area of expertise
- key ideas and/or key achievements
- limitations.

1. Make revision cards for the five people mentioned on pages 47–49:

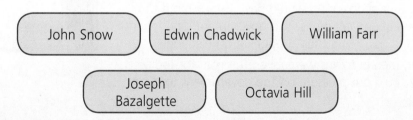

John Snow   Edwin Chadwick   William Farr
Joseph Bazalgette   Octavia Hill

2. Then use the revision cards to test yourself. Can you remember the key points about this person without turning over the card?

3. To prepare for a Section B or C question that asks you to compare two individuals, choose any two cards and write a paragraph arguing which was the most significant in improving public health in Britain in the nineteenth century.

Other factors in public health reform

Knowledge

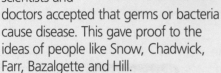

- In 1861 Pasteur published his germ theory. By 1865 most scientists and doctors accepted that germs or bacteria cause disease. This gave proof to the ideas of people like Snow, Chadwick, Farr, Bazalgette and Hill.
- As a result of this knowledge more people were willing to pay for the increased provision of clean water, public toilets and effective sewers.

Education

The electorate had been growing in size since the 1832 Reform Act. In 1884 the vote was given to workers in rural areas. Voters were becoming increasingly educated. More and more people could therefore read about current affairs, including the health of the people, medical reports and recommendations. Such people could themselves apply pressure to the government to bring about reform.

Pioneering local councils

- Birmingham and Leeds led the way in cleaning up their streets in the 1860s and 1870s, long before legislation forced them to.
- Such actions were often a result of pressure being applied by local newspapers demanding that politicians do something to clean up towns and cities.
- In 1870 a Leeds firm got a court order preventing sewage being pumped into the River Aire and in 1874 a sewage treatment works was built.
- Birmingham Council pioneered an approach known as 'municipal socialism' and used the profits from the local gas corporation to pay for improvements in street cleaning, paving and lighting.

Technology

Ideas about making improvements to public health are only part of the story. There had to be the technology to make those ideas happen. One of the results of the Industrial Revolution was that improvements had been made in such things as engineering, methods of building and construction and these were essential in the construction of public toilets and sewer networks.

Government

For centuries governments had been unable and unwilling to make public health reform compulsory.

- One reason for this was that the middle class and wealthy landowners were the only people who had the vote.
- These were the very people who would have to pay more taxes for sewers, toilets and water pipes. The government didn't want to upset them and risk losing their support at an election.
- In 1867 working men in towns were given the vote for the first time. Now they could put pressure on the government to clean up the towns.

All of these factors led to a succession of new laws in the 1870s and 1880s that were designed to improve the lives and health of ordinary people. The most significant of these was the **1875 Public Health Act** which:

- forced local councils to provide clean water, public toilets, effective drains and sewers
- forced those councils to appoint a Medical Officer of Health and other inspectors to examine and report on local public health facilities.

Write out each of the fifteen statements below and choose the most appropriate word or phrase in each statement, crossing out the options you think are incorrect. Each one also contains a deliberate mistake which you need to find and correct.

Statement	What's the mistake?
1. Towns grew very slowly in Britain between 1750 and 1850 because of the French Revolution/Industrial Revolution/Agricultural Revolution.	
2. Conditions in the streets were delightful as there were no laws governing standards of education/lighting/hygiene.	
3. Diseases like typhus, dysentery and measles spread rapidly in the overcrowded conditions/countryside/public baths.	
4. After 1837/1848/1875 all births, baptisms and marriages had to be recorded.	
5. In 1838 Doctors Arnott, Kay and Jones researched living conditions among the wealthy/middle-class/poor people in London.	
6. Bubonic plague is a deadly disease spread by infected butter/miasma/contaminated water.	
7. When Dr Shaw studied cholera in 1854 he found that most deaths occurred in the area around Wembley/the Broad Street pump/the River Thames.	
8. Cholera originated in America and first came to England in 1347/1831/1854.	
9. The author of the 1824 'Report on the Sanitary Conditions of the Labouring Population' was Edwin Chadwick/William Farr/William Gladstone.	
10. The idea that the government should interfere in people's lives is based on capitalism/environmentalism/*laissez-faire*.	
11. The ideas of Edwin Hardcastle formed the basis of the 1848 Public Health Act/London sewer network/1875 Public Health Act.	
12. The 1875 Public Health Act was an improvement on the 1832 Act because it was shorter/voluntary/compulsory.	
13. The man who designed Birmingham's sewer network following the 1858 'Great Stink' was William Farr/Joseph Bazalgette/ Edwin Chadwick.	
14. Liverpool Council used the profits from the local gas company to fund street lighting/traffic lights/road signs.	
15. When Robert Koch published his germ theory in 1861 people finally began to realise that dirt, disease, ill health and poverty were unrelated/connected/important.	

A 1d question, or a Section B or Section C question, on public health might ask you about the factors involved in improvements in public health. You should know about the role played by:

Government(s)   Individuals   Science and technology

To help you prepare for such a question work through the **Revision task** on the right.

1. For each of the factors **Government**, **Individuals**, and **Science and technology**, give three examples of that factor impacting on the development of public health.

2. Now give each example a score between 1 and 5 depending on how much you think it contributed to public health reform: a score of 1 means your example made a small contribution; a score of 5 would represent a major contribution.

3. Add the three scores for each factor; the highest score (out of 15) means you think that factor made the most significant contribution to public health reform.

1.9 Public health since c.1900

By 1900 life expectancy had started to rise. Towns were cleaner than in 1800. But there were still major health problems. The sick, unemployed and elderly received no long-term help. Those with no help had to go to the workhouse run by the local council. The Liberal Party won the 1906 general election. It began a series of reforms to tackle these problems and improve public health. These reforms were the basis for the welfare state and improved conditions for children, the elderly, the sick and the unemployed throughout Britain.

Key content

- The Liberals and social welfare reform
- The creation of the National Health Service

The Liberals and social welfare reform

Revised

The Liberal Party argued that social reform would make Britain's workers more efficient and the country would be more prosperous. The reforms would therefore pay for themselves and also create the wealth needed to re-arm to meet the growing dangers of twentieth-century warfare.

A healthier workforce was needed because the British economy seemed increasingly uncompetitive. Towards the end of the nineteenth century Britain's share of world trade was declining by comparison with its industrial rivals, Germany and the USA.

Policies to battle unemployment, old age and ill health

The following social reformers were instrumental in influencing government policy through the results of their research.

Key person

Benjamin Seebohm Rowntree

- Seebohm Rowntree was an industrialist and philanthropist.
- He was inspired by Booth's work and carried out his own survey in York. The results were published in a book, *Poverty, a Study of Town Life*, in 1901.
- His findings showed that about 29 per cent of people in York were living in poverty, almost the same proportion as Booth's London study. This helped show how the problem of poverty affected other cities apart from London.
- He became close friends with David Lloyd George and thus influenced the Liberal Party's reforms.

These ideas influenced politicians like **Lloyd George** and **Winston Churchill**. They were also impressed by the example of Germany where a system of insurance against sickness and accident as well as a system of old age pensions had existed since the 1880s.

Lloyd George spoke of the government's moral responsibility to help the poor. Churchill thought that social reforms would win votes.

Key person

Charles Booth

- Booth was a philanthropist who was highly critical of statistics to do with poverty.
- He set out to investigate the East End of London and found, with his research team, that 35 per cent of people were living in poverty – higher than the figure of 25 per cent (claimed by H.M. Hyndman, the then leader of the Socialist Party).
- His research, *Labour and the Life of the People*, was published in 1889 and he continued to research the living conditions of the poor until 1903.
- One of his proposals was to introduce old age pensions.

Key person

William Beveridge

- Beveridge was an economist and an expert on unemployment benefits.
- His report on 'Social Insurance and Allied Services' to the government proposed that workers should pay national insurance each week, so that poor and unemployed people could receive benefits.
- His proposals eventually provided the basis for the modern welfare state, including the National Health Service (see pages 54–55).

Social welfare reforms introduced by the Liberal government

Group	Act	Effect
Children	*Provision of School Meals Act, 1906*	Local council had to provide school meals.
	School Medical Services Act	Ordered the medical inspection of schoolchildren. By 1911 it showed that one-third of schoolchildren needed medical treatment.
Old people	*Old Age Pensions Act, 1908*	Helped people over 70 who earned less than £21 a year by giving them a pension of 5 shillings (25 pence) a week. Pensions were introduced in 1909, and by 1912 nearly 1 million people were claiming them.
Workers	*Workmen's Compensation Act, 1906*	Forced employers to compensate employees in dangerous jobs for accidents at work.
	National Insurance Act, 1911 (Part 1)	Everyone between the ages of 16 and 70 paid 4 pence into a national fund to which the state and employer added another 5 pence. This money would then pay for medical care of the sick.
Unemployed	*Labour Exchanges Act, 1909*	Unemployed people were helped to find work.
	National Insurance Act, 1911 (Part 2)	Introduced compulsory unemployment insurance. Workers paid a regular contribution into the fund. The unemployed received 35 pence of benefit for the first fifteen weeks in any one year.

The limitations of the Liberals' social reforms

- The free school meals were not compulsory so many local councils did not provide them.
- Old age pensions were only applied to those who had worked.
- Labour exchanges did not create jobs so the problem of unemployment persisted.
- Under the National Insurance Act medical treatment was available only to the wage earner and not to his family.
- Contributions to the National Insurance Scheme were relatively high for poor people.
- Benefits paid out under the National Insurance Scheme were not enough for many families to live on and were stopped after a few weeks.
- During 1908 the Liberals lost support to the challenge of the Conservatives and the increasingly popular Labour Party.

Revision tasks

1. Copy the diagram on the right and add notes to show the reasons why the Liberal government introduced so many social welfare reforms.

2. **a)** Create a new diagram of your own with drawings and add notes to illustrate what was done for each of the groups of people in the table above.

   b) In a different colour add a note about the weaknesses of the actions taken for each group.

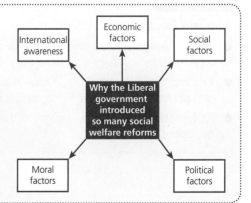

The creation of the National Health Service

During the Second World War (1939–45) many people thought that more should be done to help the poor and that health care should be available to everyone. The government invited Sir William Beveridge, who had been involved in the 1911 National Insurance Act, to investigate what could be done. In 1944 Beveridge recommended a National Health Service, providing health care that was free at point of use for everyone and funded through taxation.

Reactions to the Beveridge Report, 1944

Some people were very enthusiastic about the idea of a National Health Service (NHS) but there was opposition:

- Doctors thought they might become government employees and lose the freedom to choose treatments and their right to charge fees for seeing patients.
- Some local councils and charities objected to the government taking over the management of their hospitals.
- Some people thought that poverty and sickness were the result of idleness and therefore a person's own fault. As the NHS was a free service, people were afraid the poor and sick would take advantage of it and, worse, get used to the state looking after them. It would only discourage them from working hard, and increase their dependency on the state.

The benefits of the National Health Service

In 1945 a Labour government came to power, committed to implementing the Beveridge Report. The Minister of Health, Aneurin Bevan, brought in the National Health Service in July 1948. It introduced:

1. **Free treatment for patients**. Before the NHS was introduced some 8 million people had never consulted a doctor in their lifetime as they could not afford the fees.
2. **National ownership of hospitals**. Government funded NHS equipment, research and the development of new drugs. Money was also used to rebuild old hospitals and to build new ones.
3. **Doctors were paid by the government** but also able to charge for some private work.

As a result, life expectancy in Britain has improved, with more people living longer and fewer women dying as a result of childbirth.

Key person

Aneurin Bevan

- Aneurin Bevan was the son of a Welsh coal miner who had started work underground aged thirteen.
- Working for the miners' union gave him an understanding of poverty and sickness and inspired him to become an MP in 1929.
- As Minister for Health he brought in the NHS and overcame the opposition of the doctors.

Limitations to the National Health Service

The NHS has come under increased pressure to provide services. This is because the population has grown, the range of treatments has increased due to scientific and technological discoveries, costs have risen and people expect more. People are also living longer. This is partly due to the success of the NHS but it also adds to the demands on its services. In order to cope with these demands, there are now some limitations to the original principles of free health care for all people:

- Some services are **paid for**, e.g. adults are required to pay for dental treatment, eye tests and for prescriptions.
- Some services are so **oversubscribed** it takes time to get them, e.g. cancer treatments.
- Other services are **prioritised**, whereby each NHS trust decides which treatments should be readily offered based on evidence of effectiveness and good use of taxpayers' money.
- Some services are **not offered universally**, e.g. fertility treatment may not be funded by the NHS in some areas of Britain.

Exam tip

Questions on public health in the twentieth century may ask you to compare the Liberal welfare reforms with the National Health Service.

Complete the essay plan below to help you answer this kind of question:

Which of these changes had the bigger impact on the health of the people?

- The Liberal welfare reforms
- The National Health Service

Paragraph 1	The state of public health in c.1900 with some examples
Paragraph 2	Examples of the Liberal welfare reforms
Paragraph 3	Successes of the Liberal reforms
Paragraph 4	Limitations of the Liberal reforms
Paragraph 5	The Beveridge Report and the origins of the NHS
Paragraph 6	Achievements of the NHS
Paragraph 7	Problems with the NHS provision
Paragraph 8	Conclusion [based on paragraphs 2 to 7]: I think _____ had the greatest impact on public health in the twentieth century because _____

2 The American West, 1840–95

2.1 The Great Plains and the Plains Indians

When white people began to explore North America they found that the centre of the continent was a vast area of grassland stretching from the Appalachian Mountains in the east to the Rocky Mountains in the west, and from the Canadian border in the north to Mexico in the south. These Great Plains were home to over 30 different Native Indian tribes who were to play an important part in the history of the American West.

> ### Key content
> - The geography of North America and the Great Plains
> - The beliefs and way of life of the Plains Indians

The geography of North America and the Great Plains

Revised ☐

The difficulty of living on the Plains

The environment of the Plains presented several problems to anyone who wanted to live there.

- **Climate**: the Plains were hot in the summer (up to 40°C) and very cold in winter (well below 0°C).
- **Food**: there were few sources of food on the Plains.
- **Resources**: there were no trees on the Plains to provide wood for heating, cooking, shelter and to act as a barrier to the high winds that occurred there. There was very little water.

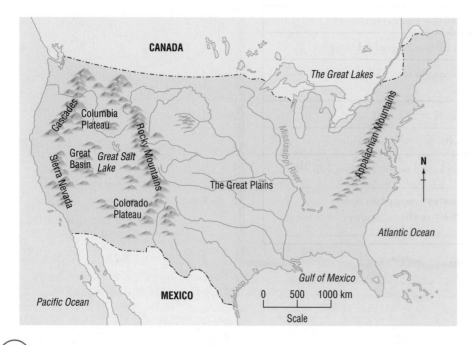

Values and beliefs: Respect for nature

1. **Resources**: Indians did not waste resources. They took only what they needed and did not spoil the land.

2. **The land**: Indians respected all life and the land. They lived in harmony with nature and their environment. The land was seen as a living thing and could not be owned. The land was seen as mother to the Indians so ploughing the land was like ripping their mother's breast. Some areas like the Black Hills were very holy for the Indians.

3. **Spirit world**: Plains Indians were very spiritual people. They believed in the Great Spirit (Wakan Tanka) who created the world. All things – animals, plants, rocks, rivers – had spirits. These spirits could influence their lives.

4. **Visions**: the spirit world could be contacted through visions. Young men wanted their first vision because from this experience the medicine man would give them their adult name. Women could make contact with the spirit world when they reached puberty.

5. **Circles**: circles were important to the Sioux as they believed life was a circle from birth to death. The circles in nature of the sun, moon and sky were echoed in the circles of their **tipis**, their village and their councils.

6. **Dances**: they danced to celebrate success and ask the Great Spirit to help the tribe. The whole tribe was brought together in the dance of hope (Buffalo Dance), of inspiration and guidance (Sun Dance), or celebration (Scalp Dance). In 1876 before the Battle of the Little Bighorn, Sitting Bull did a Sun Dance for four days before he had a vision of a great victory.

> **Key term**
>
> **Tipi** – a tent for the Plains Indians to live in.

Shelter: The tipi

1. **Assembly**: the tipi was an easily assembled and repairable home for the **nomadic** way of life.

2. **Lightweight**: it could be moved quickly to follow the buffalo. It was made of buffalo skin.

3. **Weatherproof**: it was waterproof, stable in wind; cool in summer and warm in winter.

> **Key term**
>
> **Nomadic** – always on the move, not settling in one place to live.

Warfare

1. **Fighting**: the Plains Indians usually fought in small groups. They tried to take horses or women from their enemies but not land, which they did not believe could be owned. They would raid other villages, steal horses or seek revenge for attacks they had suffered. The Indians did not fight in the winter when the snow made movement difficult.

2. **Bravery**: the Indians did not think it was heroic to die in battle as that only made it harder for a warrior's family to survive. With this in mind Indians believed in '**counting coup**'. If this was witnessed by other Indians then the warrior who did it gained a reputation for bravery which increased his warrior status. The feathers worn in the Indians' headdresses showed their victories and skill in battle.

3. **Scalping**: young men wanted to prove how brave they were and took scalps as evidence of their fighting skill. The Plains Indians believed that if they took a scalp then their enemy would not enter the afterlife.

> **Key terms**
>
> **Counting coup** – an act of bravery, for instance, touching an enemy, dead or alive, with your hand or coup stick. Coups were battle honours that were recounted and celebrated by the tribe.
>
> **Scalp** – to remove the skin and hair from the head of an enemy.

Food and resources: The buffalo

1. **Food**: the buffalo provided fresh meat which could be preserved (jerky and pemmican). The Plains Indians were nomadic **hunter-gatherers**.

2. **Resources**: all parts of the buffalo were used to provide what they needed. Skin – clothes, tipi, footwear, saddles, other utensils; bone – arrowheads; tendons – ropes. Nothing was wasted.

3. **Respect**: the Indians respected the buffalo. The heart of the buffalo was seen as the soul of the animal; they often buried it to bring new life to the herd.

> **Key term**
>
> **Hunter-gatherers** – people who hunted for food and collected food that grew or appeared naturally such as wild vegetables, eggs and honey.

Transport: The horse

1. **Hunting**: horses allowed Indians to find buffaloes and hunt them more efficiently than on foot.

2. **Transport**: horses transported the Plains Indians' homes and possessions. They used a **travois** which was dragged behind the horse. It was loaded with their possessions.

3. **Wealth**: Indians measured their status and wealth in horses. Horses were a main cause of disagreements between tribes.

4. **Horsemanship**: horses transformed hunting and warfare. Horsemanship was much admired by Indians.

> **Key term**
>
> **Travois** – tipi poles tied together with a skin between them to form a sledge that was dragged behind the horse. The Indians would place their belongings on the travois.

Decision-making and government

1. **Chiefs**: chiefs were the best hunters or fighters so the Indians' survival was guided by the experts in the tribe. Chiefs were respected for their spiritual power, experience and wisdom.

2. **Councils**: each tribe was made up of several bands. Councils decided when they would go to war. The council had representatives from each band but they were not bound by its decision. The warriors were an important group whose views were taken into account.

3. **Decisions**: decisions were taken after all men had had their chance to speak. If a warrior did not want to follow the chief's decisions he did not have to.

Work: Roles within the tribe

1. **Different roles**: men and women each had their own role in the tribe.

2. **Men**: men hunted, made decisions and defended the camp.

3. **Women**: women prepared food, made clothes, had children, and looked after the tipi. As the men could be killed hunting or defending the tribe there were often more women than men. A warrior might have more than one wife (**polygamy**) to share the work and make sure the tribe survived.

4. **Children**: children were the future of the tribe; they were taught and cared for by the extended family – the older members of the tribe, uncles, aunts.

5. **Old people**: old people were respected by the Indians for their experience and wisdom. However, everyone in the tribe accepted that sometimes the old and the weak had to be left behind to die (**exposure**) so that the rest could survive by following the buffalo.

> **Key terms**
>
> **Polygamy** – marriage to more than one person.
>
> **Exposure** – the practice of leaving old and sick people behind to die.

This task will help you in your thinking about a Question 2c or 3c – an example of which is in the **Exam practice** box that follows. Copy and complete the table below:

Aspect of Indian life	Why was it important?	Rank order of importance
The buffalo hide/skin		
The horse		
The tipi		
Polygamy		
Wakan Tanka		
The chief		
Counting coup		

Exam practice

This is an example of a Question 2c or 3c from Section B.

'Without the buffalo the Indians would not have been able to live successfully on the Great Plains.' How far do you agree with this interpretation of why the Indians were successful at living on the Plains? Explain your answer. **(12 marks)**
SPaG: **(4 marks)** *(AQA 2012)*

Answers online

Exam tip

The iceberg question

This type of question is called an iceberg question because the interpretation (the statement) highlights the buffalo as a factor (but excludes other factors). However, the question is really about all the factors which explain why the Indians were able to live successfully on the Plains. Other interpretations could be put forward which focus on the other factors – they are the part of the iceberg below the water.

The best answers will have:
- several short paragraphs, each explaining a different factor
- a conclusion that answers the question: in the light of these other factors, how convinced are you by this interpretation?

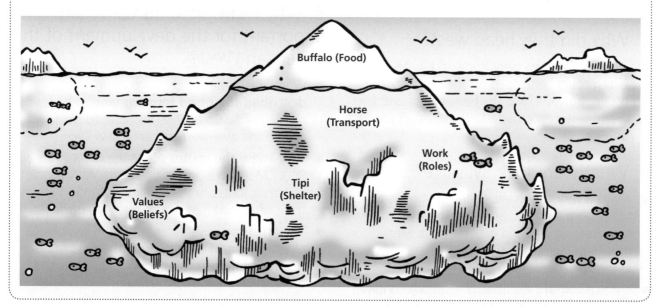

2.2 Early settlers in the Far West

The first white people who reached the Great Plains believed the harsh climate and lack of resources meant that the area was useless and uninhabitable. As a result the Great Plains were shown on maps as the Great American Desert. This did not apply, however, to the far west where the coastal plains of California and Oregon, as well as the Rocky Mountains, were to be the destinations of several groups of settlers in the first half of the nineteenth century.

Key content

- **M**ountain men
- **M**igrant farmers
- **M**ormons
- **M**iners

Revision tip

Remember the four 'M's!

Mountain men   Revised ☐

1. Who were the mountain men?

Mountain men such as Jim Bridger and Jim Beckworth hunted and trapped animals for their fur. Fur hats were very fashionable in the American East and Europe in the first half of the nineteenth century. As a result a lot of money could be made trading furs. Most mountain men worked for fur trading companies but free trappers worked for themselves and got the best price they could.

2. When did they head west?

At the height of the fur trade between 1815 and the mid-1830s there were over 3000 trappers in the Rocky Mountains.

3. Why did they head west?

The Rocky Mountains were home to elk, bear and fox which could be trapped for their fur. Most important, however, was the beaver as beaver skin hats were very popular as a fashion item in the east of America.

4. What were their lives like?

- It was a very **tough** life. Bears and hostile Indian tribes were a constant danger. They had to deal with freezing cold and extreme heat. Many mountain men did not last more than a few years in the wilderness.
- It was a **solitary** life. Their only human contact was often with Indians. Once a year, however, they met with traders and Indians at a huge meeting called a 'rendezvous' where they traded furs.

- They lived and dressed like the Indians with whom they traded. They had a **mixed relationship with the Indians** – Jim Bridger married one but Jeremiah Johnson fought them.

5. What happened to the mountain men?

By 1840 fashion had changed and beaver skin was replaced by silk. As a result, the fur trade declined in importance. In 1826 there were 600 trappers in the Snake River Valley in the Rocky Mountains; in 1846 there were less than 50.

6. Why were the mountain men important for the development of the American West?

- When they returned east, mountain men **described the good farming land** to be found on the Pacific Coast. This encouraged many people to travel west to start a new life.
- They **knew the routes** across the Great Plains and Rocky Mountains and so helped the early migrants plan their routes to the Pacific coastlands. Wagon trains often had a mountain man as a guide.
- The American government used the knowledge of the mountain men to **print the first mass-produced maps** of the Rocky Mountains and the trails through them. This also encouraged westward migration.
- They were the **first white people to make contact** with the Plains Indians.

Some people who moved west did not like certain aspects about where they lived. These were reasons that **pushed** them west. Sometimes there were things that attracted people to the West. These were **pull** factors. For most people, it was a *combination* of **push** and **pull** factors that made them move to the West.

Copy the table below and fill it in for the mountain men. Fill in the rest of the table as you read through the sections on the migrant farmers, Mormons and miners.

Migrant group	When they moved west	Push factors	Pull factors
Mountain men			
Migrant farmers			
Mormons			
Miners			

Migrant farmers

Revised

1. Who were the migrant farmers?

These were families who left their homes in eastern America to head across the continent to farm the Pacific coastlands of Oregon and California. Each family had its own covered wagon and usually joined with others to form a wagon train.

2. When did they head west?

The first group set off for the West Coast in 1843 and over the next few years thousands of men, women and children were to follow their example.

3. Why did they head west?

- There was **plenty of unoccupied land** on the Pacific Coast.
- In 1837 there was an **economic depression** which hit the eastern states hard. Banks failed, people lost their savings and unemployment was high.
- In 1842 the government passed a law (the Pre-emption Act) saying that anyone who squatted on a 160-acre plot of land for over a year could **buy the land at a cheap rate** before it was offered for general sale.
- Mountain men described the **rich, fertile farming land** that lay beyond the Rocky Mountains.

- **Land was becoming scarcer and more expensive in the East** as more immigrants arrived from Europe.
- In the past there had been disputes between the USA, Spain and Britain over who owned the Pacific coastlands. As a result, the US government was keen to encourage as many Americans as possible to settle there. This would **strengthen the American government's claim** to the area.
- The government also encouraged the belief in **Manifest Destiny**.

Key term

Manifest Destiny – this phrase had been first used by the journalist John L. O'Sullivan in 1845 and meant that white Americans believed that God wanted them to settle the whole continent. Therefore they were doing God's will by heading west.

4. What was the journey west like?

Travelling the thousands of kilometres to California in a wagon train pulled by oxen at about 3 km an hour could take up to eight months. Many wagon trains set off from Independence on the Missouri River.

There were important decisions to make **before they set off**:

When to start?
Most left in early April. Any earlier and there would not be enough grass for their animals. Any later and they might get trapped in the Rocky Mountains by winter snow. This happened to the Donner Party who left in May 1846 with disastrous results.

Which route to take?
After crossing the Plains, families could follow the Oregon Trail to the north or head further south across the Rocky Mountains to California. The Donner Party tried to make up for their late start by leaving the main trail for a shortcut and this contributed to their being trapped in the Rocky Mountains.

Who should lead the wagon train?
Early wagon trains were made up of 20–30 families each with their own wagon but later there could be as many as 200. Appointing an experienced captain who knew the route and could keep the wagon train together and under control was vital.

What supplies to take?
Everything that a family needed for the journey and to start a new life on the West Coast had to be taken with them. Supplies could be bought at some forts along the way but prices were high. Most wagons were packed so full that families had to walk.

Once the journey began there were many difficulties and dangers:

WEATHER

- Travellers could face **torrential rain, tornados, hail and sandstorms, freezing cold and scorching heat**.
- **Snow blizzards** in the Rocky Mountains were a particular danger for those who left Independence late in the year. Trapped in deep snow, the Donner Party decided to camp for the winter but animals and humans died as their food ran out. Those who survived only did so because they ate their travelling companions who had died.

ACCIDENTS

- **Broken wheels** had to be repaired with whatever was available or be abandoned.
- Accidents ranging from **accidental gunshot wounds** to **broken limbs** had to be dealt with.

> ### Revision tip
>
> The initial letters of the five dangers on pages 62–63 spell out **WAIST** – a handy way to remember them!

INDIANS

- Some Indian tribes were **friendly** and wanted to be paid as guides or to trade but others were **hostile**.
- The Gould family, travelling west in 1862, came across eleven wagons which had been **plundered** by Indians and their families killed.

SICKNESS

- Poor hygiene and little medical help meant diseases such as **cholera and dysentery** could sweep through a wagon train, killing many.
- In 1844 Henry and Naomi Sagar both died of **camp fever** leaving seven orphaned children.

TERRAIN

- **Rivers** could be wide and fast flowing. Wagons and animals could be swept away. Many migrants drowned.

- Although flat and featureless, **the Plains took weeks to cross**. They lacked surface water and supplies could run out so migrants often suffered from thirst and hunger.

- The Rocky Mountains and Sierra Nevada were perhaps the greatest challenge, coming when the migrants were already exhausted after months of travel. Wagons had to be hauled up narrow, steep mountain passes with ropes and pulleys.

- Between the two mountain ranges, those heading south to California had to cross an **80-km-wide desert called Death Valley**.

Revision task

1. Copy this diagram of a wagon wheel. It should have five spokes.

2. In each of the five sections between the spokes draw an image or images to represent one of the dangers facing the migrant farmers.

3. Ask another person if they can identify the dangers from your drawings. How could you improve your diagram to make it more effective?

4. The five headings could be written in the correct place around the rim of the wheel.

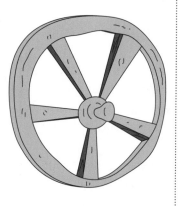

5. What happened to the migrant farmers?

Although about 34,000 people died on the trails between 1840 and 1860, the majority successfully reached Oregon or California and began their new lives. Although many came to farm the land they were accompanied by those who became shopkeepers, priests, politicians, doctors, lawyers and all the other occupations needed to build communities. With rapidly growing populations both California and Oregon were admitted into the Union by 1859.

Mormons

Revised

1. Who were the Mormons?

They were a religious group formed by Joseph Smith in 1831. From 1834 their official name was the Church of Jesus Christ of the Latter Day Saints. Their aim was to build a 'holy city' or **Zion** in America.

2. When did they head west?

They moved west in stages:

Stage 1: In 1837 they moved from **Kirtland** in Ohio to **Missouri**. In 1839 they moved from **Missouri** to **Nauvoo** in Illinois.
Stage 2: In 1846 they moved from Nauvoo across the Great Plains to the shores of the Great Salt Lake in the Rocky Mountains where they built **Salt Lake City**.

Revision task

As you work through the section about the Mormons, make your own timeline showing the main events. Mark the following dates and describe what happened:

- 1831
- 1837
- 1839
- 1845
- 1846
- 1847
- 1848
- 1857
- 1858
- 1877
- 1896.

3. Why did they move west? Stage 1

When they tried to build their holy city in eastern America at Kirtland, Nauvoo and in Missouri they were driven out by the non-Mormons.

Why were the Mormons persecuted?

General reasons	Specific reasons
• They practised polygamy, which was against Christian beliefs.	**In Kirtland**
• Mormon numbers increased rapidly wherever they settled, leading to fears that they would take over.	• The Mormons had their own bank but in 1837 it collapsed during a financial crisis. Many non-Mormons lost all their money.
• They believed that they were God's chosen people and thought of themselves as special.	**In Missouri**
• Non-Mormons thought that they were being 'looked down on' by the Mormons who didn't mix with them or gamble and drink.	• Missouri was a slave state but the Mormons opposed slavery.
• Mormon leaders believed that they should have political power and that everyone should follow their laws.	• The Mormons had the Danites who were their own secret police force.
• Non-Mormons were jealous of the economic success of the Mormons who worked hard and reinvested profits in their businesses.	**In Nauvoo**
• Mormons did not believe in individuals owning property but thought that it should be held in common by the church.	• The Mormons were allowed their own army and laws but this independence frightened non-Mormons.
• Mormons were friendly with the Indians.	• Joseph Smith was hoping to become US president. Non-Mormons were afraid that the Mormons would take over America.

Revision task

Copy the table below and write the reasons why the Mormons were persecuted into the correct column.

Religious reasons	Political reasons	Economic reasons	Other reasons

Exam tip

Reworking information in a table like this can help you remember it. It could also be a way of organising the information in an exam answer.

4. Why did they move west? Stage 2

In 1845 Joseph Smith was killed by a mob of non-Mormons. **Brigham Young** was chosen as the new leader and he made the decision to move the Mormons across the Great Plains to build their 'city of god', **Zion**, on the shores of the Great Salt Lake in the Rocky Mountains. He chose the Great Salt Lake because:

● It was an **uninhabited desert area** which no one wanted.

● It was **far away from the East** where the Mormons had been persecuted.

● This part of the Rocky Mountains was owned by Mexico so was **beyond the control of the American government**.

5. Why did the Mormons succeed?

In April 1847 Young set out with a specially chosen pioneer band to lead the way to the Great Salt Lake and start work there. On 24 July 1847 they finally reached the Great Salt Lake and built Salt Lake City which is still the headquarters of the worldwide Mormon Church. They succeeded for two reasons:

Reason 1: Planning the journey
Brigham Young carefully organised the movement of over 15,000 men, women and children across the Plains to the shores of the Great Salt Lake. He:

● made sure that **wagons were built and food stored** during the winter of 1845–46

● sent an **advance pioneer band** to set up the first staging post in Iowa called the Camp of Israel; here Smith organised the rest of the journey

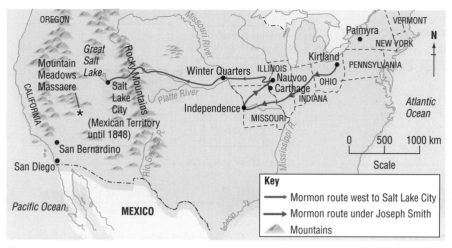

↑ **Map showing Mormon movements**

- divided the Mormons into **smaller groups of wagons**, each of which was led by a captain, and contained craftsmen like carpenters and blacksmiths

- insisted on a **strict daily routine** with punishment for those who broke the rules

- taught them how to **travel in columns** and form **defensive circles**

- built **Winter Quarters** by the Missouri River where they could rest during the winter of 1846 and prepare for the final stage of the journey.

Reason 2: Planning the settlement
They found solutions to the problems they faced when trying to build a permanent settlement at the Great Salt Lake.

Problem	Mormon solution
How was the land to be shared out between families without any disputes?	• There was to be no **private ownership of land** – instead it would all be under church control. • The church would **give out land according to family size**. • Land would be confiscated if not farmed properly.
How could crops be grown with few streams and only salty water in the Great Lake?	• There was to be **no private ownership of water**. • **Irrigation channels** were built that carried water through everybody's land.
How could homes be built in an area with little wood?	• They learned to build houses using **adobe** (sun-dried clay bricks).
How could the Mormons become self-sufficient (not rely on anyone else for anything)?	• Brigham Young set up the **Perpetual Emigration Fund** which helped pay for Mormons to travel from all over the world to Salt Lake City. • Many of these emigrants had the skills necessary to achieve self-sufficiency.
How could they become prosperous in such a barren, isolated area?	• Travellers who passed through their lands had to pay **tolls**. • Young negotiated that the **transcontinental railroad** should pass to the north and south of Salt Lake City which helped trade.
Young had set up an independent Mormon area beyond American government control. In 1848, however, Mexico handed the whole area over to the United States. How could the Mormons achieve a better political relationship with the American government and non-Mormons?	• Young wanted his area to become a Mormon state called '**Deseret**' but the US government refused. Instead the Territory of Utah was created with Young as governor. Although they were meant to follow US laws, Mormons ignored these. • Relations worsened and led to the **1857 Mountain Meadow Massacre** when 140 emigrants travelling to California were killed. The Mormons blamed Indians but they themselves were believed to have been involved in the massacre. • A full-scale war seemed inevitable but in 1858 the American government backed down. The Mormons would be allowed to live their own way if they accepted a non-Mormon governor. In practice, Young was still the real leader. • After Young's death in 1877 there was further compromise. The Mormons abolished polygamy and in 1896 Utah was accepted as a state.

Copy the diagram on the right (or design your own) and, alongside each of the boxes, explain what the problem was and how it was solved. You could use different colours for the problems and solutions.

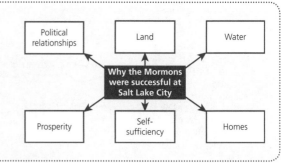

Political relationships — Land — Water

Why the Mormons were successful at Salt Lake City

Prosperity — Self-sufficiency — Homes

Miners

Revised

1. Who were the miners?

They were men searching for gold.

2. When did they head west?

The first miners arrived in 1848. However, it was 1849 that saw the real rush happen so that by the end of that year there were 90,000 miners in California alone. As a result they became known as the '49ers.

3. Why did they head west?

In January 1848 James Marshall was building a watermill at Sutter's Fort in the foothills of the Californian Sierra Nevada when he discovered gold. In December 1848 newspapers in the East began to print stories of picking up gold from the ground and making a fortune in a day. Soon thousands from eastern America and other countries were travelling to California by the overland route or by sea around Cape Horn. The California gold rush had begun!

4. What were the effects of the gold rush?

- **Stagecoach routes, the telegraph and railroad** all headed across America to California because of its growing population.
- **San Francisco** developed as a major port. It also became an important financial and industrial centre rivalling New York.

- After the first wave of miners had been and gone, **permanent towns** developed, with shopkeepers, farmers, traders and doctors all helping to settle the Far West.
- The **gold** mined in California helped make America wealthy and a leading trading nation.
- **Racial tension and conflict increased** as white Americans, Mexicans, Chinese and black Americans were thrust together in competition for gold. The Native Indians of California and Oregon were wiped out mainly as a result of the arrival of the miners.
- Mining towns sprang up quickly without any planning or services provided for the miners. They were squalid, male-dominated places where gambling, drunkenness and prostitution were common. **Law and order was virtually non-existent** so **claim-jumping** (taking someone else's mine) and murder were widespread.

5. What happened to the miners?

Only a lucky few made a fortune by finding gold. Most miners put up with terrible working and living conditions but never 'struck it rich'. All surface gold had gone by the early 1850s and many miners drifted back home again. Others headed to new gold fields in Nevada, Dakota and Arizona where the process began again.

Exam practice

This is an example of Question 1e from Section A.

1. Why did white Americans travel across the Great Plains before 1850? **(10 marks)**

Answers online

Exam tips

1. The best answers will include five or six detailed reasons why the early settlers moved west and a conclusion which explains which of those were the most important reasons.

2. Read any exam question very carefully to decide if it is asking you about people who travelled **across** the Great Plains (mountain men, miners, migrant farmers and the Mormons) or those who settled **on** the Great Plains (homesteaders).

2.3 Cattlemen and cowboys

The first white people to reach the Great Plains believed that the land was of no use to them but this huge area of natural grassland became home to one of the most successful industries in the American West – cattle ranching. The cowboy, who was central to cattle ranching, was one of the most famous figures in the American West.

Key content

- The development of the cattle industry
- The life of a cowboy
- The cowboy on the Long Drive
- The cowboy on the open range
- The cowboy on small fenced ranches

The development of the cattle industry

Revised ☐

There were four stages in the development of the cattle industry in the American West.

Stage 1: Cattle ranching in Texas

- Cattle were first brought to America by **Europeans** in the fifteenth century.
- By the nineteenth century cattle ranching was well established in **southern Texas,** which was **governed by Mexico**. The area was ideal as it had a **suitable climate** and **plenty of water** which resulted in **good grass** for the cattle (Texas Longhorns).
- **Texas Longhorns** were big animals with tough, thick hides and great stamina. The steers (males) had horns up to 2.1 metres long.
- The cattle roamed freely on the **open range** (large areas of grassland with no fences).
- In 1836 Texas won its **independence** from Mexico. Texans took over the ranches from the Mexicans.
- Between 1861 and 1865 most Texans went off to fight in the **American Civil War**. During this time the Longhorns had continued to breed and their numbers had increased to almost 5 million.
- The Civil War **destroyed the economy** of Texas so there was no market for the Longhorns in the South. Their price in Texas was as low as $4 a cow.

Stage 2: Long Drives north

- In the growing northern industrial cities there was a **large demand for beef**. Texan ranchers could get $40 a cow there, which meant that they could make huge profits. Driving a herd of 3000 Longhorns north could result in a profit of $30,000.
- Attracted by these prices, Texan ranchers began driving their cattle hundreds of kilometres north across the Plains to these new markets. These were the **Long Drives**.
- There were **four main trails** heading north – the Sedalia Trail, the Chisholm Trail, the Western Trail and the Goodnight–Loving Trail.

Key person

Charles Goodnight

- Charles Goodnight began ranching in Texas in 1856 and by 1860 had a herd of 180 cattle.
- His herd had increased to 5000 by the time he returned to Texas after the Civil War.
- In 1866 he teamed up with another rancher, **Oliver Loving**, to drive 2000 cattle north to Fort Sumner. There they could be sold to the government to feed starving Navaho Indians.
- Despite a lack of water on the trail and the threat of Comanche Indian attacks, Goodnight only lost 300 cattle on the trail and was able to make a huge profit.
- Goodnight and Loving extended the trail, which was named after them, further north to Denver and into Wyoming.
- Goodnight also invented the chuck wagon, which was a wagon adapted to carry the food and cooking equipment needed on the Long Drive.

- At this time **railroads** were being built westward across the Plains and these cattle trails connected with towns on the railroads. In this way the cattle could be transported quickly to the cities of eastern America.

- **Cow towns** grew up where the trails met the railroads. These were places where the Texan ranchers could trade their cattle with the northern buyers. Abilene, Dodge City and Wichita were cow towns.

- The period after the development of Abilene and the other cow towns was known as the **Beef Bonanza** because over 4 million cattle had been processed there by 1885.

- Despite the big profits made, there were fewer Long Drives by the mid-1880s. There were several reasons for this:

  ○ Increasing numbers of people were settling and farming on the Plains and their homesteads blocked the cattle trails.

  ○ These homesteaders were hostile to the ranchers driving their cattle north across their lands. The Longhorns carried the deadly Texas fever which could kill the homesteaders' own cattle.

  ○ Indians were given land by the American government, which straddled the trails. The Indians began to make the cowboys pay for crossing their land.

  ○ The Longhorns were very valuable so cattle rustlers and Indians would steal cattle on the Long Drive.

  ○ As more and more cattle were driven north, the grass along the trails became scarce and of poor quality. As a result the Longhorns would lose weight and so lose value.

- Instead of rearing cattle in Texas and driving them north across the Plains, ranchers began to keep their cattle **on the Plains themselves**.

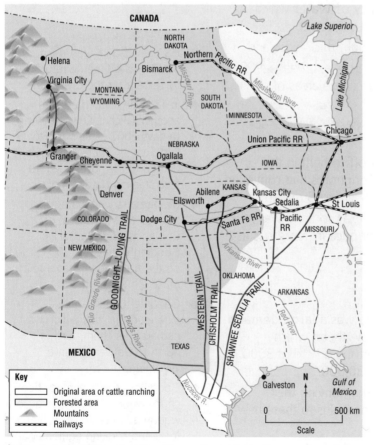

↑ **Map of the Plains showing the main cattle trails**

Key person

Joseph McCoy

- Joseph McCoy was a cattle trader from Chicago.

- He was the first person to realise the benefits of a cow town where ranchers and traders could meet.

- He bought a small undeveloped frontier town on the Kansas Pacific Railroad called **Abilene**.

- At Abilene he built cattle-pens, offices, a hotel and saloons. He also spent $5000 on advertising.

- Abilene was a great success and by 1871 over 70,000 cattle a year were processed at the cow town and then sent on by rail to the East.

Stage 3: Open range ranching on the Great Plains

- The ranches were made up of unfenced land called **open ranges**.

- These ranches covered **hundreds of thousands of acres** over which the grazing cattle wandered freely.

- Some of these ranches were so big and their owners so powerful that they were known as **cattle barons**. By 1885 just 35 cattle barons owned 8 million hectares of range, and owned nearly 1.5 million cattle.

- No one owned the land but each rancher had '**range rights**' which included the right to reserve a water supply for his cattle. There were vague boundaries agreed between neighbouring ranches.

- The cattle baron Charles Goodnight invented the '**crazy quilt**', which involved buying small patches of land scattered over a large area so that he could effectively control all of it.

- With cattle wandering freely and no clear markers as to where one rancher's land ended and another's began it could be **difficult to distinguish** each ranch's cattle.

- This problem was solved by using a **red-hot branding iron** to burn a distinctive symbol or mark on each animal. Each ranch had its own distinctive brand mark which told the rancher which were his cattle.

- Disputes over these range rights and unbranded cattle could lead to serious conflicts known as **Range Wars** (see section 2.5, page 81).

- In the late 1870s Gustavus Swift, who owned a meat packing business in Chicago, developed a **refrigerated train wagon**. This meant that meat could be transported all over the USA and even abroad, giving higher profits.

- From 1880 to 1885 open range ranching was very successful as it produced cheap meat for the consumer and big profits for the ranchers. However, in the late 1880s open range ranching ended. The reasons were:

  ○ **Overstocking**: the Plains now contained vast herds of cattle and there wasn't enough good grazing for them all. This meant that the cattle lost weight and, therefore, value.

  ○ **Falling demand**: Longhorn cattle produced tougher meat which was becoming less attractive to consumers who preferred the higher quality meat produced by the new cross-bred cattle. These cattle couldn't be successfully bred on the open ranges where they mixed freely with the Texas Longhorns.

  ○ **Range Wars**: as more farmers settled on the Plains there were frequent conflicts over land and water between the ranchers and farmers, e.g. the Johnson County War of 1892 (see page 81).

  ○ **Weather**: the cold winter of 1885–86 was followed by a very hot summer during which the grass shrivelled up and streams ran dry. Worse was to come with the severe winter of 1886–87 during which temperatures fell to –60°C and cattle could not reach the grass through the deep snow. Some ranchers lost three-quarters of their herds and many went bankrupt.

  ○ **Technology**: in 1874 **Joseph Glidden**, an Illinois farmer, invented **barbed wire** which allowed land to be fenced cheaply. Earlier, in 1854, an American engineer, Daniel Halladay, had invented a successful **wind pump** which allowed ranchers to pump up water from underground.

Key person

John Iliff

- Born in 1831, John Iliff's early career in the West was as a trader selling goods to the farmers and miners travelling across the Plains.

- He realised that he could make more money as a cattle rancher than a trader and began building up his own herd.

- He bought cattle from settlers travelling to Oregon as well as from Oliver Loving so that by 1866 he had a herd of 35,000.

- He found that the hardy Texas Longhorns could survive the harsh winters on the northern Plains so set up his ranch in Colorado.

- He won contracts to supply beef to the construction gangs building the transcontinental railroad in 1867 and to Sioux Indians on their reservation near Fort Laramie.

- He was so successful that he was known as 'the cattle king of the northern Plains'.

- Iliff experimented with cross-breeding Longhorns with Hereford bulls brought from England. The resulting cattle produced better quality meat and more milk. They weren't as hardy as the Longhorns but this was no longer as important because they did not have to survive the Long Drives.

Stage 4: Ranching on small fenced farms

- By the end of the 1880s open range ranching had been replaced by **small farms which were individually owned**.

- These farms were **fenced with barbed wire** and got their water from **wind pumps**.
- Ranchers could experiment with **cross-breeding** as their cattle could now be kept separate.

Revision task

Cattle ranching went through several stages and it is important to know why these changes happened. Make a list of the reasons for the changes underneath the arrows in the table below.

STAGE 1 Ranching in Texas		STAGE 2 The Long Drives		STAGE 3 The open range		STAGE 4 Fenced farms	
	→	Reasons for the change	→	Reasons for the change	→	Reasons for the change	

Revision task

Explain the importance of each of the following for cattle ranching on the Plains.

Event/Development	Importance
The American Civil War	
The Goodnight–Loving Trail	
Cow towns	
John Iliff	
Railroads	
The invention of barbed wire	

The life of a cowboy

Revised

It was the cowboy's job to look after the herds of cattle either on the Long Drives or on the open range.

The cowboy, both real and fictional, became one of the most well known characters in the American West, appearing in paintings, photographs, books, films and TV series. Their lives, however, were often very different to the one shown in the media. The kinds of people who became cowboys were:

- **young men** looking for adventure and an exciting life. Some were criminals escaping justice in the East
- **ex-soldiers** who found it difficult to settle back to civilian life after the end of the American Civil War in 1865

- **black ex-slaves** – as many as 25 per cent of cowboys in some areas – who had few other prospects; there was also slightly less discrimination in the West
- many **Mexicans and Indians** who already lived in the region.

Regardless of their background, most cowboys came from lower social classes and the pay was poor. The average cowboy earned approximately a dollar a day plus food and, when near the home ranch, had a bed in the bunkhouse.

The cowboy's clothes and equipment were very practical and designed for the conditions in which he worked.

Bandana: a large cotton scarf that could be used to protect the back of the neck from the sun, or the face from dust storms, could become a sling or bandage.

Chaps: made of leather and protected the rider's legs while on horseback, especially when riding through thorny vegetation or while working with the cattle.

Slicker coat: a coat made of waterproof oilskin which was long enough to protect the saddle as well as the cowboy from the weather.

Stetson: hat with a wide brim to protect the cowboy from the sun, rain and snow.

Boots: had high tops to protect the lower legs, pointed toes to help guide the foot into the stirrup and heels to keep the foot from slipping through the stirrup while working in the saddle. They were usually worn with detachable spurs.

Gloves: made of soft and flexible leather for working purposes, yet protected the hands when using barbed wire and the lariat or clearing scrub.

Lariat or lasso: made of thin leather and used for catching the cattle.

Saddle: designed so that the cowboy could work for many hours in a secure seat over rough ground or when moving quickly while herding the cattle.

Revolver: was more of a status symbol than a useful weapon as few cowboys were accurate shots.

Horse: was generally on the small side, with a short back, sturdy legs and strong muscles. It had to be intelligent, calm under pressure and have a degree of 'cow sense' – the ability to anticipate the movement and behaviour of cattle.

As ranching changed, so did the life and work of the cowboy.

The cowboy on the Long Drive

Revised

- Long Drives from Texas could last up to **two months,** during which the cowboys would be up at around 4a.m. and not finish until after dusk. A cowboy might work for **24 hours** if it was also his turn to guard the herd at night.

- The average herd of cattle on a Long Drive was about 3000 and would need a team of about ten cowboys. Within this team there were specific jobs, such as the **trail boss** who was in charge as well as **swing men** who rode at the side to keep the herd together. **Drag men** were at the rear as were **wranglers** (usually the youngest cowboys) whose job was to look after the **remuda** (spare horses). The team also included a cook, who drove the **chuck wagon**, and was a valuable member because he was not only in charge of the food, but also medical supplies.

- Much of the cowboy's work was **tiring, boring and routine** but there were **dangers** on the Long Drive:

  ○ **Stampedes** were particularly dangerous for cowboys as they could be knocked off their horses and trampled to death.

  ○ **Weather** could be extreme with scorching hot winds, torrential rain or hailstorms.

  ○ **Arguments** with other groups. As homesteaders spread across the Plains their farms blocked the trails. Some Indians wanted payment for crossing their lands while others tried to steal cattle. Rustlers would also steal cattle because they were valuable.

  ○ **Terrain** could also be difficult due to rivers with fast flowing currents or quicksand.

- When the cowboys reached a cow town at the end of the Long Drive they would drive the herd through the town to the stockyards firing their guns. They would be paid and, after months of exhausting and dangerous work, would have free time. As a result, cow towns had a reputation for violence, lawlessness, drunkenness, prostitution and gambling.

Revision tip

The initial letters of the dangers described above spell out **SWAT** – a handy way to remember them!

The cowboy on the open range

- At the centre of each ranch on the open range were the buildings where the cowboys lived, including the **bunkhouse**.
- However, as the Longhorns could wander long distances on the open range, cowboys spent most of their time **on horseback** travelling around the Plains keeping an eye on the cattle.
- In winter they would '**ride the line**' around the far boundaries of the range to make sure that the cattle were not in difficulty in the snow or from wild animals. The cowboys would live in tents.
- **Spring** was a busy time. This was when cattle were rounded up and newly born calves branded. With cattle wandering over such huge areas, this **round-up** could take two or three months.
- The round-up was **dangerous** for the cowboys because the Longhorns had been roaming freely on the open range and were like wild animals. The cowboys needed all their skill with the lariat and their horse to deal with a fully grown steer.
- In late summer cowboys would drive cattle to the **market** to be sold.

The cowboy on small fenced ranches

Keeping cattle on fenced ranches changed the job of the cowboy:

- There were **no more Long Drives**. Large-scale round-ups or branding cattle weren't necessary any more.
- **Fewer cowboys** were needed on the Plains.
- Their **lives were more settled** as they lived on the ranch all year round, putting up and repairing fences, moving cattle between fields and feeding them hay in winter.

Revision task

Make notes about cowboys under the following headings: Clothes and equipment; On the Long Drive; Who became a cowboy; On the open range; On fenced ranches.

Exam practice

This is an example of a Question 2b or 3b from Section B.

1. Using Source F and your own knowledge, explain why the work of a cowboy was difficult and dangerous. **(8 marks)** *(AQA 2011)*

Answers online

Exam tip

The source will give you one thing to write about when answering the question, in this case, the difficulty and danger of roping a steer.

To get a high mark you will need to use your own knowledge to write about **and explain** at least two other relevant factors or reasons. In this example you could also write about stampedes, and the threat from Indians and settlers.

Source F: *Cowboys lassoing a steer*

2.4 Farming on the Great Plains: The homesteaders

Before the 1860s most white Americans travelled **through** the Great Plains to get to the West Coast. From the 1860s white people began to **settle** and **farm** on the Great Plains. These people were the homesteaders. There was much land on the Plains that was free and could be made into a small farm or homestead.

Key content

- The homesteaders and their reasons for going west
- Government actions to encourage settlement
- The problems of farming
- Solutions to the farming problems
- The problems living on the Great Plains
- Solutions to the problems
- The lives of women on the Great Plains

The homesteaders and their reasons for going west

Revised

1. White Americans

- Most homesteaders were white Americans. They saw the Plains as offering opportunities; **land was free** under the US government's **Homestead Act of 1862**, if it was farmed for five years.
- They came from the **overcrowded East** where farmland was scarce and expensive in the 1860s.
- When the American Civil War ended in 1865 **thousands of ex-soldiers** wanted a new challenge and start so they moved to the Plains.

2. European settlers

- Railroad companies advertised the land they had been given by the government and **sold it cheaply** to thousands of homesteaders after 1870.
- Many Europeans came to the Plains from Britain, Ireland, Sweden, Germany, Denmark, Norway, Holland, France and Russia to **escape poverty**.

3. Religious groups

- Religions which were **persecuted** saw the Plains as a place to set up their own communities.
- These groups included the **Mennonites from Russia** in the 1870s, and the **Amish from Germany and the Netherlands** who moved to the Plains in the 1870s.

4. Black Americans

- **Thousands of ex-slaves** were free after the defeat of the South in the American Civil War.
- They were **poor and often persecuted by whites**; the Plains offered them a chance for a new life and to get land and freedom. In 1879, 40,000 black ex-slaves went to Kansas.

Revision task

Why did people become homesteaders?

Make your own copy of the push/pull table (see section 2.2, page 61) and add notes about the **push** and **pull** factors which made people move onto the Plains. This will help you answer a common question 1e in the examination: **Why did people move onto the Plains?**

- Sometimes there were things that attracted people to a life on the Plains. These were **PULL** factors.
- Some people who moved onto the Plains did not like something about where they lived at that time. These were reasons that **PUSHED** them onto the Plains and away from where they lived.
- Most people had a *combination* of **PUSH** and **PULL** factors that made them move to the Plains.

Government actions to encourage settlement

Revised

Building the railroad

- **The Pacific Railways Act, 1861,** led to the construction of the **Transcontinental Railroad**.
- The government paid the railroad companies to build it by giving them 6400 acres of land on the Great Plains for every mile of track they built.
- The railroad companies **advertised** in America and Europe that there was cheap land available in the West. Newspaper adverts exaggerated the quality of the land but they succeeded in bringing in thousands of homesteaders.
- The land was sold cheaply by railroad companies offering ten-year loans.

Promoting Manifest Destiny

- This phrase was first used by journalist John L. O'Sullivan in 1845. It meant that the white Americans believed that they were **intended by God** to settle the whole continent. Although O'Sullivan was describing the flood of settlers to California and Oregon, the idea took hold and was applied to the homesteaders of the 1860s.
- The US government wanted **total control** over the land of the USA, and so encouraged settlement of the Plains. The Acts it passed and the actions of the US army in the Plains Wars made it easier for the nation to achieve its 'Manifest Destiny' and take over the whole continent.
- The US government encouraged the homesteaders to believe that their **sacrifices** on the Plains were part of the nation's work towards its Manifest Destiny.

Passing Acts

- The US government wanted settlers to move onto the Plains in huge numbers. But speculators had claimed vast areas of land and then sold the land to potential homesteaders. The prices put settlers off going to the Plains. The Homestead Act would stop this happening.
- The **Homestead Act, 1862**, was a law passed to help the settlers afford and make a success of their homestead on the Great Plains. According to the Act, all American citizens were entitled to 160 acres of land on the Plains for a fee of just $10. They had to live on the land for five years, and then it was theirs permanently. The five-year term would stop speculators from claiming the land.
- Some homesteaders complained that 160 acres was not enough to support a family because of the poor quality of the soil and the difficulties of farming. The **Timber and Culture Act, 1873**, gave homesteaders another 160 acres of free land if they planted 40 acres with trees.
- Later on the government followed these Acts up with the **Desert Land Act, 1877**, which gave the homesteaders the right to more land.

Dealing with the Plains Indians

- The US government signed a succession of treaties with the Plains Indians from the 1830s onwards. Each treaty **reduced the amount of land available** to the Plains Indians, and granted more to the American settlers, e.g. 1st Fort Laramie Treaty 1851, 2nd Fort Laramie Treaty 1868.
- During the 1860s and the 1870s the US army fought **a series of wars** with the Plains Indians tribes with victories for US army leaders such as General Sherman and Custer.
- By the end of the 1880s the Plains Indians had been totally defeated and **the US army had moved them off their lands onto the reservations**, leaving the land free for the homesteaders to settle and farm.

Revision task

Read the following government actions and describe what **effect** each would have on homesteaders and settlement.

- Making treaties with the Indians
- Fighting wars against the Indians
- Giving land to the railroad companies
- Putting the Indians on reservations
- Advertising land in newspapers
- Passing laws allowing land to be bought cheaply
- Encouraging the railroad to be built
- Speaking of Manifest Destiny

The problems of farming

- 'The Great American Desert' was not suited to agriculture. Annual **rainfall** on the Plains averaged 38 cm. Rainwater soon evaporated.

- No one had farmed the Plains before. There were thick deep grass roots of up to 10 cm in tangled clumps. Iron **ploughs broke** when used on the Great Plains.

- The types of maize and wheat used were suited to the mild, damp climate of the East. They did **not grow** well on the dry, hot Plains.

- The Homestead Act, 1862, gave the homesteaders 160 acres of land each. Homesteaders could not feed their families with only 160 acres. Crops did **not produce enough** due to the harsh climate and lack of water. Many homesteaders simply gave up their plots.

- Homesteaders' crops were damaged by wandering cattle. Crops were **trampled** by buffalo herds until the 1870s.

- Homesteaders did almost everything by hand and they had **no machines**. Work was physically hard and never-ending. Spare parts for broken machines were expensive and difficult to get from towns or the East.

- Accidental fires started by a spark or broken glass were a disaster. Unless the **fire** could be stopped quickly by beating, it soon spread.

- Swarms of grasshoppers plagued the Plains in 1871, 1874 and 1875. The **insects** could eat a homesteader family's entire crop in just a few hours, leaving farmers with nothing to eat or sell.

Revision task

Complete your own version of the diagram below.

- Match up the complaints of the homesteaders about farming on the Plains with the details of the problems they faced.

- Read the section below and add a solution next to the relevant problem on your diagram.

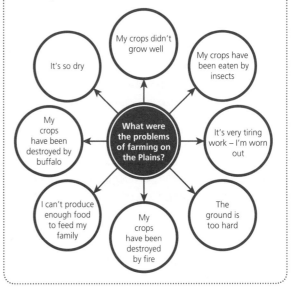

Solutions to the farming problems

1. **Barbed wire**: **Joseph Glidden** invented barbed wire in 1874 which was cheap, simple fencing. Barbed wire let homesteaders overcome the shortage of trees on the Plains, to mark their land/ claim and to keep stray cattle and buffalo off.

2. **Sodbuster**: in 1830 an Illinois blacksmith, **John Deere**, made a steel plough for one of his neighbours. This stronger plough cut through the Plains soil. This 'Sodbuster' plough was very popular with homesteaders.

3. **Government Acts**: the **Timber Culture Act, 1873**, provided homesteaders with wood for fires, building and trees that acted as windbreaks. The **Desert Land Act, 1877**, gave homesteaders more land – an extra 640 acres. If they put in irrigation after three years homesteaders could buy it for $1 an acre. By 1877 homesteaders could own up to 960 acres of land – enough to survive on the Plains.

4. **Dry farming and the wind pump**: a new method known as 'dry farming' trapped the rain. Every time it rained or snowed, the homesteaders ploughed their land. In 1854 Daniel Halliday invented and patented a wind pump; this allowed water to be raised from 30 to 120 feet underground. Although it was expensive at first, the price fell to $25 by the 1880s.

5. **Fire breaks**: there was no real solution to this problem except to be careful to avoid fire. Some farmers left gaps in crops to stop the spread of fires but land was scarce.

6. **Pesticides**: there was no solution to insect attacks until the 1900s when pesticides were available. Homesteaders could pick the insect larvae off their crops. However there was no hope if a swarm of grasshoppers arrived.

7. **Turkey Red**: this was a type of wheat that grew well in the extremes of temperature and lack of rainfall. It had been brought by Russians moving onto the Plains after 1874.

8. **New machines and railroads**: from the 1870s railroads provided cheap, fast transport from eastern states to the Plains. Machinery and spare parts were supplied to farmers at lower prices. New machines such as reapers, binders and threshers made farming on the Plains much easier because homesteaders could farm more land and harvest more crops.

The problems of living on the Great Plains

Revised

1. Homesteaders needed to build houses but there were very few trees. **Wood** from the East was expensive.

2. Limited supply of **water**. Water was a precious resource. Homesteaders were lucky if they had a stream, river or lake nearby. Most had to travel daily to a waterhole or stream and get water in a bucket by hand. This could be many miles away. Water had to be used sparingly as replacing it was hard work.

3. The homesteaders lived hard and tiring lives. It was a constant struggle to keep clean, warm and fed. Diets were often poor in years of bad harvests. **Disease** was common in sod houses, especially amongst children.

4. As nights on the Plains were **cold** and winters were freezing they needed fuel to heat homes and for cooking.

5. From the early 1860s the homesteaders faced the risk of **Indian attacks**. Tribes had moved onto reservations after the 1851 Fort Laramie Treaty but often they did not have enough food or supplies. They could not hunt buffalo or follow their traditional migration patterns. This led to outbreaks of violence in the 1860s and 1870s.

6. The **sod houses** they built were **dirty**. Sod walls cracked and flaked in hot weather, leaving dirt in the house. The roofs leaked dirty water into rooms. The floors were dirty and wind blew in dust. Walls and floors were infested with lice, which crawled over the homesteaders as they slept.

7. **Climate**: winters were long, freezing and snowy; summers were very hot. The vast open spaces of the Plains encouraged dust storms, high winds and tornadoes. These damaged homes and equipment.

8. **Isolation**: homesteaders lived on their 160-acre plots, far from their nearest neighbours and miles from the nearest town. There was little company or social life. Homesteaders were cut off from their families back in the East or in Europe.

Revision task

Complete your own version of the diagram on the right.

- Match up the complaints of the homesteaders about life on the Plains with the details of the problems above.
- Some of the problems are connected with others. Explain how they are connected.
- Read the next section and then add any solutions to your diagram in a different colour.

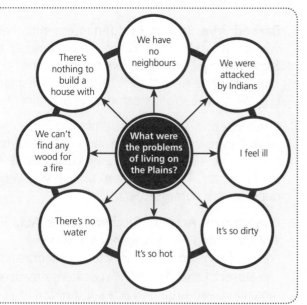

Solutions to the problems

- **Community involvement and letters**: homesteaders wrote regular letters home. In time and as towns grew, neighbours would help each other in times of crisis. Women worked as midwives and teachers, and church or community groups organised social functions.

- **Constant hard work**: the dirt was tackled by constant work – sweeping, removing fallen mud lumps. Some homesteaders whitewashed walls which was smarter than mud, but still leaked.

- **Wind pumps**: by the 1870s, wind-driven pumps were available so water could be more easily obtained.

- **Buffalo dung**: homesteaders copied Indians and used buffalo dung (known as **chips**) as fuel for their fires. Women collected buffalo chips in a wheelbarrow. When extra trees that had been planted grew after 1877, they had wood. Towards the end of the nineteenth century homesteaders were able to buy coal from the railroad.

- **Cures**: homesteaders had to rely on their own medicine when they were sick. Women were responsible for this. Knowledge was shared and passed on from mother to daughter. Women worked together in a community when sickness was present to ensure that people were cared for.

- **Sod houses**: the homesteaders made bricks from sods of earth cut from the Plains. In time, and after the railroad was complete, homesteaders could afford to bring more wood onto the Plains to build houses.

Revision task

Homesteaders were often attracted to the West by pictures like the one on the right.

1. Why would it be attractive?
2. Why was it inaccurate?
3. Make notes around the picture about:
    - features that were attractive to settlers
    - features that might have been exaggerated.

Exam practice

This is an example of a Question 2c or 3c from Section B.

'The new farming methods were the main reason white people were able to settle on the Great Plains.' How far do you agree with this interpretation of why white people were able to settle on the Plains? Explain your answer.
(12 marks)
SPaG: (4 marks)

Answers online

Exam tip

This is a common type of question in Section B of the examination. You will recognise it as an **iceberg question** (see page 59), where you have to deal not only with the factor named in the interpretation but with the other factors too.

Plan an answer with a paragraph for each of the following five factors:

1. The new farming methods and technology
2. The removal of the Plains Indians
3. The railroad
4. Government laws
5. The work and determination of the homesteaders

In your conclusion answer the question: in the light of these other factors, how convinced are you by this interpretation?

A view of life on the Plains
Source A: *An early settler's home*

This painting was made in 1868 by Fanny Palmer. Fanny Palmer travelled widely on the Plains. Her paintings were popular in the East and were reproduced in magazines.

A different view of life on the Plains
Source B: *Dr Cass G. Barns' description*

In 1878 Dr Cass G. Barns and his wife arrived in Nebraska. He described his house, as follows:

'We had a good house by June but the joints between the sods needed new fine clay occasionally to keep the rainwater from trickling through. When it rained the roof leaked dirty water onto our bed and I would wake up with water running through my hair. It was not completely the fault of the sod house that contagious diseases were common. The open dug well, the outdoor toilet (or no toilet at all) shared the blame with a lack of ventilation and overcrowding. The earth floor was not possible to scrub or disinfect.'

Exam practice

This is an example of a Question 1a–c from Section A.

1. **a)** What does Source A suggest about life on the Plains? **(4 marks)**

b) What different impression of life on the Plains is suggested by Source B? Explain your answer using the sources. **(6 marks)**

c) Why do you think the sources give different impressions? Explain your answer using Sources A and B and your own knowledge. **(8 marks)**

Answers online

Exam tip

Question 1a

In the examination your knowledge and understanding will be tested by comparing two different views. Question 1a uses the word 'suggest'. So try to use your own words that sum up the mood or main message of the source(s). This can often be the same as your first impression of the picture in Source A.

Question 1b

Concentrate on the new source to begin with. Follow the same advice in the **Exam tip** given for Question 1a. Try **not** to just copy the words of Source B. Try to use your own words to sum up the mood or main message of the source.

Finally say **how** the impression you get from one source is different to the impression in the other source. The word 'whereas' is useful to join the two impressions together in one sentence: *In A it seems like the homesteaders … whereas in B the impression is that they …*

Do not try to explain **why** there is a difference yet – that belongs in your answer to Question 1c!

Question 1c

There are many things to look for when trying to explain why different people at different times have different views about history. One of the simplest ways to start explaining different views and sources is to use the **TAP** idea. **TAP** stands for:

Time: are the sources from different times in history? What knowledge do you have about the events at that time that might help explain why the sources are different?

T Time
A Author
P Place

Author: are the authors different? What do you know about the author or artist or photographer that might help you explain the view they have or the image they have produced? Who is the audience for the source?

Place: are the sources from or about different places? What do you know or can guess at that might explain why the difference in place might affect what is said, written or shown in the source?

Think about each aspect in turn in your answer and **try to connect it with the history you have learned**.

Women had many roles on the Plains. Women would:

- help the men plant crops
- make and repair clothes
- bring up the family (older sisters would help the mothers with this)
- make soaps and candles
- tend to the animals

- cook
- collect fuel
- provide for medical needs in the family (e.g. home cures)
- kill pests and dangerous animals (such as snakes).

What was life like for women on the Plains?

- Life for women on the Plains was **difficult**, particularly if they were used to a more comfortable lifestyle. Women needed to be tough and resilient in order to survive. Many ended up leaving the Plains because they couldn't cope.

- It was a lonely, **demanding** life. Women were often left home alone or with the children. Cleaning and cooking were very difficult on the Plains. This was because the buildings were made from sod and were very unsanitary. They were difficult to keep clean; insects and vermin lived in the walls which whitewashing only partly improved. Illness was common in these conditions.

- Many women moved to the Plains for jobs. There were saloon girls drawn by the prospect of easy money but there were also those women such as teachers who helped civilise the West. At first their lives were very **different** to the ones they had in the East; it shocked many of them. There were often few toilets or comforts. There was a lot of responsibility in their jobs. For example, a schoolteacher would have to teach a large group of children of mixed ages on her own.

How important were women homesteaders?

Women were the ones who did all of the food storage, housework, child bearing and raising and also some of the farming and animal care. So much work was done without machines and needed physical strength and endurance. There were a few homesteaders, both male and female, who lived alone on the Plains. Usually for a homestead to be successful an entire family was needed – a husband, wife and children.

Exam tip

The picture given in this exam question will contain some information to help you answer the question. Use that as a starting point and explain how it helps to answer the question. For higher marks you must add some of your own knowledge.

For this question you should read again about the problems of living and farming on the Plains and then study the source. The following bullet points will help get you started:

- physical work
- new skills needed
- dangers on the Plains.

Source F: *A homesteader collecting buffalo 'chips' for fuel*

Exam practice

This is an example of a Question 2b or 3b from Section B of Paper 2.

2.b) Using Source F and your own knowledge, explain why life on the Plains was hard for homesteader women. **(8 marks)**

Answers online

2.5 Law and order

The American West during this period is often called 'The Wild West' and is shown as an extremely violent and lawless area. Some of this is exaggerated but keeping law and order could be difficult in the West.

Key content

- The types of crime committed in the American West
- The Range Wars
- Gangs and gunslingers
- How the problems of law and order were dealt with

The types of crime committed in the American West

Revised

1. **Bank robbery**: the James–Younger Gang were ex-soldiers who had fought for the southern states during the American Civil War. After the war, between 1866 and 1882, they robbed banks. They were like many *ex-soldiers who found it difficult to adjust to civilian life* after the end of the war in 1865.

2. **Cattle rustling**: *large profits could be made* from the cattle trade, and cattle roaming on the open range were easy targets as brand marks could be altered.

3. **Claim jumping** was a problem in the mining areas of the Far West. *Towns had grown up so quickly* that there was no formal system of law and order. *The government in Washington did not always see the West as important* so were not prepared to spend money on law and order.

4. **Fence cutting**: in the 1880s and 1890s homesteaders and small ranchers cut the barbed wire put up by cattle barons trying to enclose large areas of land. Crimes like this were often the result of *different groups competing for land* on the Plains and could result in **Range Wars**.

5. **Train robbery**: between 1870 and 1880 outlaw gangs such as Butch Cassidy and the Wild Bunch frequently robbed trains. In the early days of the West *there were not enough lawmen* to deal with the threat from *gunslingers and gangs* like these. Sheriffs, marshals and judges had too large an area to cover and in some cases were no better than the criminals. Henry Plummer, elected sheriff of Bannock in 1864, was, in fact, the leader of a band of robbers who carried out many crimes in the area.

6. **Horse stealing**: a serious crime because of the *value of horses on the Great Plains* and often punished by hanging. The problems of official law enforcement often led to crimes like these being dealt with by **vigilantes**.

7. **Racial attacks**: Chinese workers helping build the railways were often victims but with so many *different ethnic groups settling in the West* conflict between them was not uncommon.

Key terms

Cattle rustling – stealing cattle.

Claim jumping – Stealing land already claimed by other miners.

Range Wars – armed conflict for control of open range.

Vigilante – someone who takes the law into their own hands. Having identified who they believed was responsible for a crime, they would give out instant punishments with no proper trial. This could lead to innocent people being hanged.

8. Shootings: there was a *gun culture* in the West. Most people carried guns and believed that it was their responsibility to settle disputes themselves. Arguments could easily end in a shooting. For example, **cow towns** were seen as violent places with frequent drunken brawls and saloon fights, although some historians argue that deaths have been exaggerated.

9. Robbery by road agents: individual travellers and stage coaches were easy targets in *the vast open spaces of the West* where transport and communication was slow, making it difficult to enforce law and order.

Revision tasks

The information in *italics* in the boxes on page 80 and above explains the **causes** of lawlessness and violence in the American West.

1. Copy the diagram on the right (or design your own) and link each cause of lawlessness to one of the five factors in the outer ring. Some causes may be linked with more than one factor.

2. Using your completed diagram, which factors seem most important in causing lawlessness in the American West?

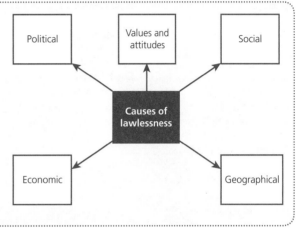

The Range Wars

Revised ☐

The crimes listed on page 80 and above were often carried out quickly by individuals or small groups but the scale of lawlessness could increase and involve significant numbers of people over longer periods of time. An example was the **Range Wars**.

What were the Range Wars?	These were armed conflicts for control of the open range. They often began with disputes over water or grazing rights and involved both farmers and ranchers.
When were they?	Mainly in the 1870s and 1880s.
What examples are there?	1. 1875–76: **The Mason County War** in Texas between German settlers and non-German ranchers. 2. 1882–92: **The Pleasant Valley War** in Arizona between cattle ranching and sheep herding families. 3. The most famous Range War was **The Johnson County War** (1889–92) in Wyoming. ● In the 1880s Johnson County in Wyoming was controlled by the powerful Wyoming Stock Growers Association, made up of large-scale ranchers known as cattle barons. ● Their control of the open range was being threatened by the growing number of homesteaders and small ranchers settling in Wyoming. ● The cattle barons blamed these homesteaders and small ranchers for a rise in rustling (taking unbranded cattle) and took the law into their own hands after 1889 by killing some of the alleged rustlers without any trial. ● In 1892 the cattle barons hired a vigilante army of Texan gunmen 'the Regulators' to sort out the rustlers once and for all. However, after attacking the KC Ranch they were forced back to their base at the TA Ranch by an army of farmers and small ranchers.
How did the Range Wars end?	**The Johnson County War:** ● Besieged by nearly 300 men at the TA Ranch, the cattle barons used their political influence to call in the US Cavalry who freed the Regulators. ● Although the Regulators were put on trial, they were never convicted. ● However, cattle barons had lost their power and influence in Wyoming where the homesteaders and small ranchers continued to farm.

Gangs and gunslingers

'Dime novels' were cheap storybooks about the American West. They were often fictional and wildly exaggerated but were extremely popular. They showed the American West as a lawless and violent place full of **gangs and gunslingers**. What was the truth about these characters?

WANTED

Example 1: Billy the Kid

Born: 1859 in New York

Occupations: cowboy, gambler, cattle rustler, outlaw

Myth and reality: very little is known about Billy the Kid's life. He did kill a man in 1877, and was involved in the Lincoln County Range War of 1878. He also escaped from prison on more than one occasion and became an outlaw. It was only after his death that biographies began to appear that exaggerated his exploits. It was claimed that he killed 21 men, while most historians agree that it was between 4 and 9.

Real name: Henry McCarty

Also known as: William H. Bonney, Billy the Kid

Died: 1881 when shot by Sheriff Pat Garrett

WANTED

Example 2: The Original Wild Bunch

Also known as: The Doolin-Dalton Gang, The Oklahoma Long Riders

Members: at various times there were as many as eleven members of the gang.

Years when active: 1892–95

Criminal activities: robbing banks, and stores, holding up trains

Myth and reality: the gang carried out eight robberies during the four years that they were together, during which at least five people were killed. In 1893 US Marshall Evett Nix was given the task of hunting down the Wild Bunch with the help of 100 specially appointed marshals. Nine members of the gang had been killed by 1898, with only two members surviving into the twentieth century.

Revision task

1. Copy the table below.

2. Using the information on the **Range Wars** and **gangs and gunslingers,** add evidence to the table that supports and contradicts the two statements about law and order in the American West.

3. Make sure that you can remember at least two examples of supporting and contradictory evidence.

Statement 1: The American West was a violent place		Statement 2: Law enforcement in the American West was not effective	
Supporting evidence	Contradictory evidence	Supporting evidence	Contradictory evidence

How the problems of law and order were dealt with

1. **W**omen played an important role in civilising the West, often as school teachers. Between 1847 and 1858 over 600 women teachers crossed the untamed frontier to bring education and some civilisation to the American West.

2. **Improved communications**: the expansion of the railways after 1869 and the development of the telegraph both meant that it was easier to enforce the law across the vast area of the West.

3. **Local government developed**: when settlers first moved west, the areas in which they settled were known as federal territories with officials sent out by the government in Washington. When a territory had a population of 60,000 it could become a state with responsibility for keeping law and order. Important decisions about law and order could now be made locally, not hundreds of miles away in Washington. They could now choose or elect their own town marshals, county sheriffs and judges.

4. **Miners' courts**: miners set up their own courts and, although it was difficult for them to deal with more serious crimes, they did settle disputes between miners and bring some kind of order to these areas.

5. **Advances in civilisation**: as local government developed, the original poor quality townships were replaced or improved with proper sanitation, water supplies and roads. All this created a more civilised atmosphere and better behaviour.

6. **Settlers and their families**: early settlements such as mining or cow towns were usually male dominated but, as more families moved west to find a better life, they were not prepared to put up with lawlessness and expected local officials to tackle the problem. For example, in 1823 the **Texas Rangers** were formed to protect settlers moving into the area, while in 1872 cowboys were banned from Abilene.

7. **Vigilantes**: although in some cases vigilantes could add to the problem of lawlessness, they could also be a force for good. It was a vigilante committee which finally brought Henry Plummer to justice in 1865.

Exam tip

The initial letters of the eight factors on page 82 and on the left spell out **WILMA'S TV** – a handy way to remember them!

Revision task

Some people find it easier to remember information when it is presented in picture form. Draw a picture for each of the solutions to the problems of law and order in the American West.

Exam tip

The best answers will look at two aspects of the source:

1. What does the **content** of the source tell us about the problem of law and order that makes it useful or not? The content of the source can be checked against your own knowledge of the topic.

2. What does the **provenance** of the source tell us about how useful, or not, the source might be? Although this question is only asking you to study one source, you can still use the TAP (Time, Author, Place) idea explained on page 78 in section 2.4 to help you.

Don't forget that this question is about how **useful** the source is. You must say how useful the source is in your answer or you will lose marks.

Exam practice

This is an example of a Question 1d from Section A.

1. How useful is Source E for understanding the problems of law and order in the American West? Explain your answer using Source E and your own knowledge. **(8 marks)**

Answers online

Source E: The front cover of a 'dime novel' describing the life of the notorious criminal 'Billy the Kid,' by the lawman who shot and killed him, Sheriff Pat Garrett. Dime novels were cheap storybooks, often about the 'Wild West' and were very popular among readers in the eastern states.

2.6 The struggle for the Great Plains

There was little conflict on the Great Plains when the first white settlers crossed them to reach the Pacific Coast and Rocky Mountains. It was only when white settlers began to settle on the Plains that the long struggle for control of the Great Plains began – a struggle that was to end disastrously for the Indians.

Key content

- Why the arrival of white people on the Great Plains led to conflict
- The American government's policy towards the Indians before 1860
- How the American government policy towards Indians changed after 1860
- The Battle of the Little Bighorn
- Why the Indians lost the struggle for the Plains

Why the arrival of white people on the Great Plains led to conflict

Revised

Reason 1: Neither Indians nor white people could understand each other's culture

Plains Indians	Living on the Plains	White Americans
Indians lived a nomadic lifestyle, moving across the Plains following and hunting the buffalo herds. They lived in tipis which could be taken down quickly.		On the Plains white Americans were mainly farmers who had to stay in one place to plant, look after and harvest their crops. They built permanent homes to live in.
Indians believed that the earth was their mother and should be loved and respected. Like a person, it could not be bought or sold.	**Attitude to land**	White Americans believed that God had given them the earth to make the most of. This meant making money by farming or mining. Land ownership, fences and farming were all part of this.
Important decisions were taken by the tribal council whose members would keep talking until all had agreed. Chiefs could not make warriors obey them.	**Government**	White Americans had laws which had been passed by the central government in Washington. Everyone was expected to obey these laws.
Indians believed in Wakan Tanka, the Great Spirit, who created the world. All things were sacred, even rocks, rivers and trees.	**Religion**	White Americans were Christians who believed in one God. They thought that it was their Christian duty to convert the Indians.
Indians gained honour in battle by counting coup and took scalps as trophies. Indians retreated quickly if they were outnumbered or thought they might be killed.	**War**	For white Americans courage meant standing up to the enemy and fighting to the last man. Death in battle was seen as an honour.
Indians practised polygamy. A man could divorce his wife by a simple announcement. Exposure meant that the weak and helpless were left to die on the Plains.	**Family life**	Most white Americans believed in monogamy and that it was their Christian duty to look after the elderly and sick.

Conclusion

White Americans saw the Plains Indians as subhuman and inferior. The Plains Indians saw white Americans as devils who ruined the earth. Both sides grew to distrust and despise the other and this led to conflict.

1. Make your own copy of the following table. Read the six statements on the right of it and write them into the correct column.

2. Opposite each comment write a brief reply from either an Indian or white American.

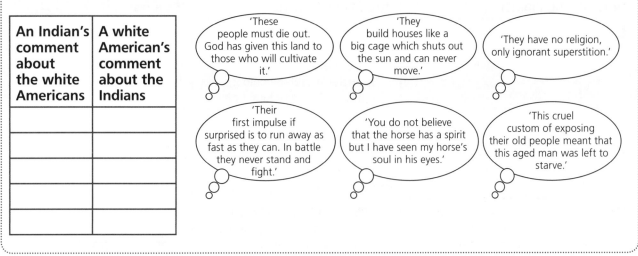

An Indian's comment about the white Americans	A white American's comment about the Indians

'These people must die out. God has given this land to those who will cultivate it.'

'They build houses like a big cage which shuts out the sun and can never move.'

'They have no religion, only ignorant superstition.'

'Their first impulse if surprised is to run away as fast as they can. In battle they never stand and fight.'

'You do not believe that the horse has a spirit but I have seen my horse's soul in his eyes.'

'This cruel custom of exposing their old people meant that this aged man was left to starve.'

Reason 2: White Americans wanted the Great Plains for their own use

- The first white people who explored the Plains saw it as impossible to live on. The land could not be farmed. There was very little wood and water. They called it 'The Great American Desert'. It looked as if the Indians would have the Great Plains to themselves and be able to continue with their traditional lifestyle.

- Unfortunately for the Indians, white attitudes towards the Great Plains were to change and they began to see the Great Plains as a valuable resource which should be exploited.

- As a result, more and more white Americans moved onto the Great Plains.

- Ranchers began driving their cattle northwards from Texas across the Plains to cow towns such as Abilene. By the 1870s ranching itself had spread onto the Great Plains. By the 1890s open range ranching was replaced by fenced ranches which changed the whole nature of the Plains.

- Finally in the late 1850s homesteaders began to move onto the Great Plains to farm. By the late 1890s virtually all of the Plains had been settled by white Americans.

Conclusion

This settlement of the Great Plains by white Americans made the nomadic life of the Plains Indians difficult. Both sides ended up fighting to keep or establish their way of life on the Great Plains.

Revision task

Copy the diagram on the right (or design your own). Alongside each of the outer boxes explain how that aspect of the Indians' way of life might have been affected by the arrival of white Americans on the Plains.

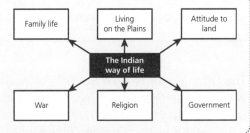

The American government's policy towards the Indians before 1860

Time	What was happening on the Plains?	Government policy towards the Plains Indians	Results
1830s	By the late 1830s mountain men and traders were crossing the Plains.	• **1830: The Indian Removal Act.** • **1834**: **Permanent Indian Frontier** established along 95th meridian (a line of longitude).	• Eastern Indian tribes moved onto the Plains. • The Indians given all of the Great Plains as **'One Big Reservation'**.
1840s	Pioneer farmers, Mormons and miners all crossed the Plains. Indians began to attack wagon trains.	Treaties signed. The Indians promised not to attack travellers in return for protection and guaranteed land, e.g. 1849 treaties signed with Comanches and Kiowas.	An uneasy peace on some of the Plains. Elsewhere, Indian attacks increased after the gold rush to California.
1850s	• 1854: homesteaders moved onto the central Plains. • 1859: miners moved into Cheyenne territory when gold was discovered at Pike's Peak.	• **1851**: **Fort Laramie Treaty** began the **Concentration** policy. • Each Indian nation given a hunting area 'for all time' away from the white trails, e.g. Sioux given the Black Hills of Dakota.	Travellers would not be attacked. The government opened up Indian land for white settlers. The Indians got guaranteed land, money and protection for ten years.

This didn't solve the problem of the worsening relationship between the Indians and the white settlers on the Plains and there were many examples of brutal acts by both sides.

Here are two examples:

The Utter Massacre on the Oregon Trail, 1860	The Sand Creek Massacre, 1864
In 1860, eight families joined together under the leadership of the Utter family to follow the Oregon Trail. On 9 September, their wagons, 44 people and 100 animals were attacked by about 100 Indians while nearing the Oregon border. The wagon train formed a defensive circle to protect the livestock. The Indians attacked, trying to stampede their animals. Finally they made friendly gestures and the white men agreed to give them food. But the Indians attacked again as soon as the wagons started to move on. Several animals and three white men were shot. The Indians attacked again in the morning and in the end 27 survivors were forced to flee and hide a short distance away. The next morning the surviving migrants continued west on foot. They rested by day and travelled at night but only twelve reached safety – the others having been killed by Indians or starved to death.	In 1864, about 600 Cheyenne, led by Black Kettle, had their camp at Sand Creek where they believed that they had been promised protection by American troops. They were peaceful and had a US flag flying. In November Colonel John Chivington arrived in the area with a regiment of 1000 volunteers. They surrounded the camp, and at daybreak on 29 November attacked, taking the Indians completely by surprise. Though Black Kettle raised a white flag and the Stars and Stripes, Chivington's regiment slaughtered over 150 Indians, including many women and children.

Conclusion

The Utter Massacre is an example of warriors staying on the warpath even when their chiefs made peace with the American government. The Sand Creek Massacre is an example of the American government breaking many of the promises and treaties that it had made with the Plains Indians. With such events happening it is not surprising that conflict worsened, with both sides seeking revenge.

1. Make a storyboard like the one below and draw a series of simple cartoons or images to tell the story of the Sand Creek Massacre.

1.	2.	3.	4.	5.

2. Now do the same for the Utter Massacre.
3. Talking about information can help you remember it better. Show your storyboards to another person. Can they understand what happened just from your images? Discuss how you could change your images to tell the story more effectively.

How the American government policy towards Indians changed after 1860

Revised ☐

Time	What was happening on the Plains?	Government policy towards the Plains Indians	Results
1860s	• Despite the promises made at Fort Laramie, Indian lands were being invaded by miners, settlers and cattle drives. • Railroad builders also wanted the Indians removed from the routes they were planning to take. • Indian attacks on railroad builders, travellers and settlers worsened.	• **1861**: **Fort Wise Treaty** set up the Sand Creek Reservation for the Cheyenne. • **1867**: Peace Commission set up by Congress which separated Indian tribes from each other on **small reservations** away from white settlers. • **1867**: **The Medicine Lodge Treaty** with the southern Plains Indians. • **1868**: **The Fort Laramie Treaty** with the northern Plains Indians. • By the late 1860s: Indians were no longer allowed to leave reservations to hunt buffalo. They were to give up their tribal ways and learn to live like white farmers. The buffalo herds were to be destroyed.	Poor conditions on the reservations led to Indian uprisings and attacks on settlers: • **1862**: **Little Crow's War** • **1863**: **Cheyenne uprising** • **1865**: **Red Cloud's War**. These ended in defeat for the Indians, often involving surprise attacks and massacres: • **1864**: **Sand Creek Massacre** • **1868**: **The Battle of Washita**. New treaties were then signed which often moved the Indians onto smaller reservations with even worse conditions.
1870s	1874: gold found in the Black Hills of Dakota on sacred Sioux land which had been guaranteed by the Fort Laramie Treaty. Miners poured into the area.	• 1875: Sioux refused to sell the Black Hills to the government. More Sioux warriors leaving their reservations. • After the Battle of the Little Bighorn, government policy was to **destroy the Plains Indians' way of life and culture** completely.	• **1876**: **the Battle of the Little Bighorn**. Custer and 225 men killed. • All Indian tribes were forced to move to reservations. Reservations placed under army control.
1880s	• By 1883: buffalo herds finally destroyed. • By 1885: all Indian tribes on reservations. • Illegal settlers moved onto Indian lands.	• **1887**: **The Dawes Act** divided the remaining Indian lands into 160-acre plots. Most went to white settlers. • 1889: President Harding opened up 2 million acres of Indian territory to white settlers, leading to the **Oklahoma Land Rush**.	Indians were to live like white farmers on individual plots of land. Reservation life was hard (poor quality land; inadequate government hand-outs; dishonest Indian agents).
1890s	• By the 1890s the Plains had largely been settled by white people. • In 1890 the government announced that the frontier was closed.	The government continued its policy of using reservations to control the Indians by destroying their way of life and culture, and making them dependent on government handouts.	• **1890**: **The Battle of Wounded Knee**. Reservation conditions led the Sioux to resort to the **Ghost Dance**. The army tried to disarm the Indians, which led to the massacre of 153 Indians.

Copy and complete the table below to create a summary of the key points of American government policy on page 87.

Government policy	Date policy started	Why the policy was started (Use brief bullet points)	Was it a success or failure?	Evidence for success or failure (Use brief bullet points)
One big reservation				
Concentration				
Small reservations				
Destruction of way of life and culture				

In an examination you would not be expected (or have time) to discuss all the events from the table on page 87 but you should be able to give some examples of events during the struggle for the Plains. The **Revision task** on the left should help you with this.

The Battle of the Little Bighorn

Revised

This was one of the most famous battles in the American West because it was a victory for the Indians and saw the death of General Custer and 225 of his men.

Examination questions usually focus on why Custer lost the Battle of the Little Bighorn.

Background

- In the spring of 1876 **an army was sent to Montana** to deal with Indians who had left their reservation.
- **General Terry** was in overall charge of the army although the plan of attack had been devised by **General Sheridan**.
- The Indians were a combined force of 12,000 Sioux and Cheyenne led by **Sitting Bull and Crazy Horse**.
- The original plan was a three-pronged attack. **General Crook** would attack from the south, **Colonel Gibbon** from the west, and **General Terry** with General Custer from the east.

Events on 25 June 1876

- Custer's scouts found a **large Indian camp**.
- Custer decided on an **immediate attack**.
- **Custer split his men into three groups** led by himself, Major Reno and Captain Benteen.

- Major Reno's attack was forced back but he was **helped by the arrival of Captain Benteen**.
- Custer and his 225 men became isolated and **were all killed**.

Who was responsible for the defeat?

The army commanders (Terry and Sheridan)?

- The plan was difficult to carry out as there was **no effective communication** between the three armies.
- No attempt was made to find out **how many Indians** there were.
- Despite knowing that **Custer had a history of disobeying orders**, Terry put him in charge of the Seventh Cavalry.

General Custer?

- His **desire for fame and a glorious victory** meant that he put his own interests first.
- He **refused the offer of extra men** and **Gatling guns**.
- He **disobeyed orders** and rode across the Wolf Mountains, arriving at the Little Bighorn a day earlier than planned.
- By marching through the night **his men and horses were exhausted**.
- He **decided to attack without waiting** for the other armies.

- He **ignored the warnings** of his Indian scouts about the size of the Indian camp.
- He **split his men** into three smaller forces.
- His **poor relationship** with Reno and Benteen made them less inclined to support him.
- Custer's soldiers only had **single-shot rifles**, which were slow to reload.

Reno and Benteen?

- They **did not help Custer** despite receiving an order from him to do so.

The Indians?

- The Indians outnumbered Custer because **several tribes had combined**.
- They were given **confidence** by Sitting Bull's Sun Dance vision of victory.

- They were **better armed** with repeating rifles.
- They fought a **pitched battle** rather than their usual hit-and-run tactics.
- They **knew the terrain**.

Bad luck?

- **Quicksand** stopped Custer from crossing the river to capture the women and children as hostages.
- Indian warriors were not out hunting but **asleep in their tipis**.
- Indians discovered a **dropped ammunition pack** and had Winchester Repeating rifles, but did not return to alert the camp, which Custer expected them to.

Exam practice

This is an example of a Question 2c or 3c from Section B.

'Custer's actions caused the defeat of the Seventh Cavalry at the Battle of the Little Bighorn.'
How far do you agree with this interpretation of why the Seventh Cavalry
lost the battle? Explain your answer.

(12 marks)
SPaG: *(4 marks)*

Answers online

Exam tip

Remember the idea of an **iceberg question** (look back to page 59). It is common to have questions about different interpretations of why the Seventh Cavalry lost the Battle of the Little Bighorn. Check your original class notes or the textbook.

Plan an answer with a paragraph for each of the following interpretations:

- The actions of General Custer
- The actions of the Indians
- The actions of Reno and Benteen
- The actions of the army commanders, Terry and Sheridan
- Luck

In each paragraph say what the event was (two to three sentences) and what importance it had in the defeat at the Battle of the Little Bighorn (two to three sentences). In your conclusion remember to comment on which factor you think was the most important. One factor has been done for you as an example.

Luck:

- It was bad luck that Custer could not get across the river to capture the women and children. The quicksand prevented him doing what he had done at the Battle of the Washita River in 1868.
- The cavalry might have used the women and children as hostages and escaped.

Why the Indians lost the struggle for the Plains

After the Battle of Wounded Knee, and despite all their efforts, the Indians had lost the struggle for the Great Plains which were now controlled by white settlers and their government. The Indians' way of life and culture had been destroyed. There are several reasons why this had happened.

Revision task

1. Copy the diagram below (or design your own) which shows important reasons why the Indians lost the struggle for the Plains. Underneath the diagram are statements explaining these reasons. Link each explanation to one of the reasons on the diagram. Some reasons have more than one explanation.

2. Highlight on your diagram the four reasons that you think are the most important for the defeat of the Plains Indians. Explain why they are the most important.

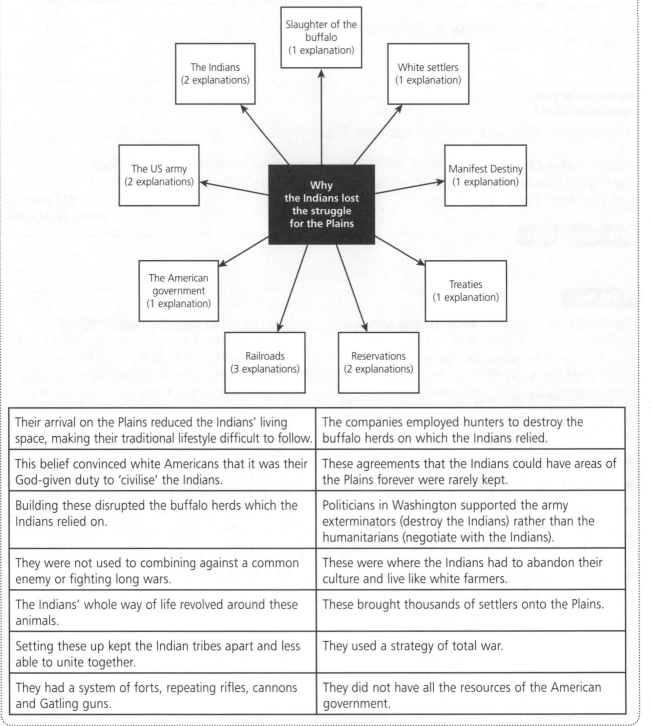

Their arrival on the Plains reduced the Indians' living space, making their traditional lifestyle difficult to follow.	The companies employed hunters to destroy the buffalo herds on which the Indians relied.
This belief convinced white Americans that it was their God-given duty to 'civilise' the Indians.	These agreements that the Indians could have areas of the Plains forever were rarely kept.
Building these disrupted the buffalo herds which the Indians relied on.	Politicians in Washington supported the army exterminators (destroy the Indians) rather than the humanitarians (negotiate with the Indians).
They were not used to combining against a common enemy or fighting long wars.	These were where the Indians had to abandon their culture and live like white farmers.
The Indians' whole way of life revolved around these animals.	These brought thousands of settlers onto the Plains.
Setting these up kept the Indian tribes apart and less able to unite together.	They used a strategy of total war.
They had a system of forts, repeating rifles, cannons and Gatling guns.	They did not have all the resources of the American government.

This is an example of a Question 1d from Section A.

1. How useful is Source E for understanding the fate of the Plains Indians? Explain
   your answer using Source E and your own knowledge. **(8 marks)** *(AQA 2009)*

Answers online

Source E: *Visions of Yesterday*

This painting is called *Visions of Yesterday*, painted by W.R. Leigh in 1931. Although he was based in New York, Leigh travelled during most summers after 1906 to the West, where he became particularly interested in painting the Plains Indians.

Exam tip

The best answers will look at two aspects of the source:

1. What does the **content** of the source tell us about the fate of
   the Plains Indians that makes it useful or not? The content of the
   source can be checked against your own knowledge of the topic.

2. What does the **provenance** of the source tell us about how
   useful, or not, the source might be? Although this question only
   asks you about one source, you can still use the TAP idea (Time,
   Author, Place) from page 78 in section 2.4 to help you.

Don't forget that this question is about how *useful* the source is.
You must say how useful the source is in your answer or you will
lose marks.

3 Germany, 1919–45

3.1 The Nazi rise to power 1: Weimar Germany

- At the end of the nineteenth century Germany was a powerful and wealthy country. In 1890 it had the second largest population in Europe, one-third of whom were under the age of fifteen. It had a strong army, as well as good welfare and education systems.

- In 1914 Germany was ruled by an emperor (**the Kaiser**) with the support of important groups in German society. The Kaiser was a strong leader and held most of the power. The imperial system of government had worked well and was supported by the middle classes. The Kaiser was ambitious for Germany, and he wished to increase its power and influence.

- However, there was criticism of his government before 1914. Germany had many trade unions

which had their own political party – the SPD or **Social Democrats** (Socialists). The Kaiser's government and the trade unions fell out when some businesses encountered hard times, wages fell and the workers went on strike. The outbreak of a (short) war was seen by some as an opportunity to unite Germany.

> ### Key content
> - How the First World War weakened Germany
> - Why the Weimar government was unpopular, 1919–23
> - Weimar successes under Stresemann, 1924–29

How the First World War weakened Germany

Revised

- The war began in August 1914. The German plans to avoid fighting the French and British in the west and the Russians in the east failed. Modern transport methods and communications meant that the German armies met opposition sooner than they expected. Neither side could strike a decisive blow. Both sides dug trenches and it was a stalemate.

- Opposition to the war in Germany split the Social Democrat opposition. The majority of Socialists (SPD) supported the war. The minority Independent Socialists (USP) did not.

- Over the next four years the war went badly for Germany. Its armies retreated. The German people suffered and many starved. Germany knew the war would be lost.

- The **Allies** (Britain, France and the USA) would not make peace unless Germany became more democratic so the Kaiser left Germany. However, he appointed Social Democrats to the government so that they would get some of the blame for the way the war ended.

- Revolution (like that of 1917 in Russia) was in the air. The German armed forces were rebelling. The SPD majority took their chance and formed a government. The new government promised elections and arranged a ceasefire (armistice). It was known as the **Weimar Republic**.

> ### Key terms
>
> **Allies** – in the First World War Britain, France and the USA worked together in an alliance.
>
> **Weimar Republic** – a republic is a government system not ruled by a hereditary ruler. After the First World War it was set up in Germany at a town called Weimar.

1. The Weimar government signed the Treaty of Versailles

The treaty seriously weakened Germany. Four main aspects deeply angered and upset Germans:

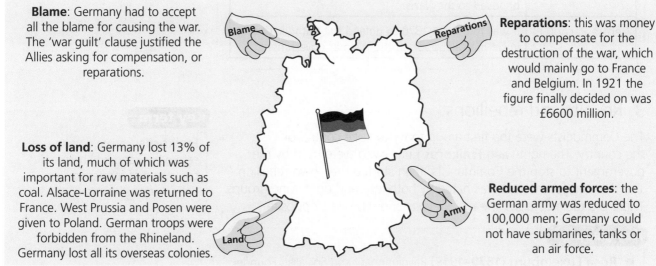

Blame: Germany had to accept all the blame for causing the war. The 'war guilt' clause justified the Allies asking for compensation, or reparations.

Reparations: this was money to compensate for the destruction of the war, which would mainly go to France and Belgium. In 1921 the figure finally decided on was £6600 million.

Loss of land: Germany lost 13% of its land, much of which was important for raw materials such as coal. Alsace-Lorraine was returned to France. West Prussia and Posen were given to Poland. German troops were forbidden from the Rhineland. Germany lost all its overseas colonies.

Reduced armed forces: the German army was reduced to 100,000 men; Germany could not have submarines, tanks or an air force.

Germans felt humiliated by the treaty. They thought that the German army had not lost the war. They blamed the Social Democrats for signing the treaty and believed that they had betrayed the army and had stabbed Germany in the back. The politicians had no choice as they did not want the war to start again and knew if it did they could not win it.

2. The new system of government was weak

In 1919 there was an election for a President to replace the Kaiser as the head of the country. A new set of rules for how the government would work were drawn up in the peaceful little town of Weimar. It was known as the Weimar Constitution.

- The system was meant to be fair but it encouraged lots of small parties.
- This in turn required politicians to be skilled at coalitions and compromise on policies.
- Decisions took time and needed discussion.
- Because of Article 48 (see the diagram on the right), it was also possible for a President to have too much power and become a dictator.

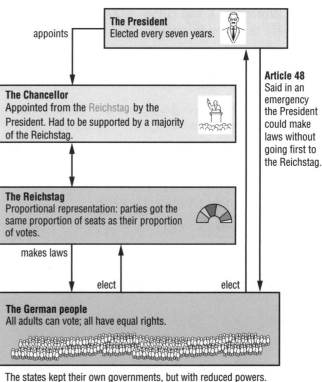

The President
Elected every seven years.

appoints

Article 48
Said in an emergency the President could make laws without going first to the Reichstag.

The Chancellor
Appointed from the Reichstag by the President. Had to be supported by a majority of the Reichstag.

The Reichstag
Proportional representation: parties got the same proportion of seats as their proportion of votes.

makes laws

elect   elect

The German people
All adults can vote; all have equal rights.

The states kept their own governments, but with reduced powers. National laws could overrule state laws.

Key terms

Constitution – a set of rules about how to govern a country.

Coalition – an arrangement in which two or more political parties agree to work together in government.

Reichstag – the German Parliament.

Social Democrats (SPD)	The largest party in the Reichstag. Strong supporter of the Weimar Republic.
Independent Socialists (USP)	A group that broke away from the Social Democrats in 1917.
Communist Party (KPD)	It was formed in 1918. Would attract new members from the unemployed in the 1930s. Strongly opposed to the Nazis.
Centre Party (ZP)	It was formed in 1870 to defend the Catholic Church in Germany. Supported the Weimar government.

3. Revolts and rebellions

The Communists were the first group to try to seize control of the country. The right-wing **Freikorps** units, who were used by the government to stop the Communists, then started their own rebellion. The Weimar government was hated by both left- and right-wing groups. There is a table detailing the main revolts and rebellions opposite.

Key term

Freikorps – military units set up by President Ebert and composed of former soldiers. They were anti-communist.

Key people

- **Rosa Luxemburg (1870–1919)** Revolutionary and Socialist. Founder of German Communist Party (KPD). Killed by Freikorps.

- **Karl Liebknecht (1871–1919)** Revolutionary and Socialist. Elected to Reichstag in 1912. Opposed war. Co-founder with Luxemburg of Spartacist League. Organised uprising in Berlin in January 1919. Killed by Freikorps.

- **President Ebert (1871–1925)** Social Democrats leader from 1917 and President of Weimar Germany until 1925.

- **Wolfgang Kapp (1858–1922)** A government official who was elected to the Reichstag in 1919. Leader of the Kapp Putsch.

Why did rebellions against Weimar fail in the years 1919–23?

- None of the rebellions were well organised enough or had enough support to overthrow the Weimar government.
- They did not offer a clear or attractive alternative to the Weimar government.
- The inflation of the 1920s did not cause as much hardship as the mass unemployment of the 1930s.
- The army did not intervene or support the rebellions.

Details of the main revolts and rebellions 1919–23:

	The Spartacist Rising	The Kapp Putsch	The Red Rising in the Ruhr	The Munich Putsch
Who was involved?	The Communists and workers (Spartacists)	Freikorps units	Workers	The Nazis
Who led it?	Rosa Luxemburg and Karl Liebknecht	Wolfgang Kapp	Communists	Adolf Hitler
When?	January 1919	March 1920	March–May 1920	8–9 November 1923
Where?	Berlin	Berlin	The Ruhr – one of Germany's main industrial areas	Munich, Bavaria, southern Germany
Why did it happen?	Communists felt that they had been betrayed by the Socialist government which had removed the Independent Socialist Police Chief in Berlin. They thought that the Social Democrats (SPD) had made a deal with the army and big business.	To reduce the number of armed men in line with the Versailles Treaty, Freikorps units were ordered by the Weimar government to disband and go home.	Workers were angry about poor conditions and low wages.	Hitler believed in the stab-in-the-back myth about the end of the First World War. He used General Ludendorff to gain more support for his cause. When the Bavarian government banned political meetings Hitler thought it was the right time to act.
What did they want?	A communist-style revolution like the Russian Revolution.	To overthrow the Weimar government.	Communists wanted revolution. Workers wanted better conditions and wages.	Hitler hoped to start a rebellion ('putsch') in Munich that would spread throughout Germany. He wanted to set up a separate government in Bavaria and then march on Berlin to overthrow the national Weimar government.
What happened?	Left-wingers seized newspaper offices, blocked streets and called for a general strike. They started a revolution in Berlin and fought to seize control of the government.	Freikorps units occupied Berlin. Kapp tried to form a government.	Following protests throughout 1919, 50,000 workers took over the factories and the supplies of raw materials.	He interrupted a political meeting where the leader of Bavaria, Gustav von Kahr, was speaking. He held everyone prisoner in the beer hall until Kahr agreed to his demands.
How did it end?	The SPD government used former soldiers (Freikorps) under Defence Minister, Gustav Noske, to fight back and crush the revolution. Rosa Luxemburg and Karl Liebknecht were killed by the Freikorps.	Although the German army refused to help, the rebellion was defeated by a general strike of German workers. Kapp fled to Sweden. Many Freikorps leaders did not join the putsch.	The army and the Freikorps stopped the rising. More than 1000 workers were killed.	In the morning Hitler expected to march triumphantly through the streets of Munich but he was met by a barrier of armed police. In the fighting that followed several Nazis were killed, Hitler was arrested and the putsch was over. Sixteen Nazis lay dead and many others were wounded. Hitler escaped but was captured two days later, charged with treason and sent to prison.

4. Germany was invaded by the French in January 1923

The Weimar government had to pay reparations. When France did not receive the payments of reparations early in 1923, French troops were sent into the industrial region of the Ruhr to take what was owed. The Weimar government called for workers not to co-operate and a campaign of 'passive resistance' followed. German industry ground to a halt.

> **Key term**
>
> **Hyper-inflation** – inflation is when the prices increase rapidly. Hyper-inflation is when this happens at an incredibly fast rate.

5. Germany was poor and Germans suffered from hyper-inflation

Partly because of the problems in the Ruhr the government printed extra money, causing **hyper-inflation**. The value of the currency, the mark, fell dramatically. The value of any money that Germans had saved seemed to vanish overnight. All Germans suffered from hyper-inflation but it hit the middle classes with savings particularly hard. They blamed the Weimar government for this problem.

> **Revision task**
>
> Here is a summarised diagram about attitudes to Weimar Germany after the war. Add notes to each branch to explain why Germans would think as they did.

Hyper-inflation:

The government becomes very short of money.

↓

The government prints more money to pay workers and to pay its debts.

1000 M   1000 M

↓

The more money printed, the less it is worth.

1000 M   100,000 M   1000 M

↓

People lose confidence in the German mark.

100,000 M   1,000,000 M   100,000 M   100,000 M

↓

Prices rise at an incredible rate (hyper-inflation).
In January 1919 one US dollar is worth nearly 9 marks.
By November 1923 one dollar is worth 200 billion marks.
At one stage an egg costs 80 million marks and a glass of beer 150 million marks.

1,000,000 M   1,000,000 M   1,000,000 M   1,000,000 M

↓

By November 1923 the German mark is worthless.

1 BILLION M   1 BILLION M   1 BILLION M   1 BILLION M   1 BILLION M   1 BILLION M   1 BILLION M

Weimar successes under Stresemann, 1924–29

Revised

Gustav Stresemann took over as Chancellor of Germany in August 1923. A lot of the credit for Weimar Germany's success should go to Stresemann.

What did Stresemann do to help Germany recover?

1. He solved the problem of the French occupation. Stresemann called off the passive resistance to the French invaders. He promised to carry on paying reparations. The French left the Ruhr and industrialists and workers could resume making profits and earning wages. But Stresemann had upset some right-wing Germans who said he had given in and was weak.

2. Stresemann introduced a new currency called the **Rentenmark**. All the old money was handed in and destroyed. The new money stopped the inflation and prices became more predictable and stable for everyone. However, the German people, and especially the middle classes, never forgot the hyper-inflation and the loss of their savings and they blamed the Weimar government.

3. Germany did a deal over its eastern borders with Russia (**The Rapallo Agreement, 1922**) which led to improved trade links. It upset the West and right-wing Germans who disliked communist Russia, but boosted the economy and helped the workers and factory owners.

4. Stresemann repaired the damage to Germany's international relations. The **Locarno Pact (1925)** promised France and Belgium that Germany would not invade and further restored Germany's international status. In 1926 Germany was allowed to join the **League of Nations** which had been created to police international agreements after the war and supervise the Treaty of Versailles. Many Germans thought that Germany's international status had been regained. However, some Germans disliked this as the League of Nations was associated with the Treaty of Versailles and France.

5. Stresemann reduced Germany's reparation payments. He negotiated the **Dawes Plan** with America in **1924** which reduced and rescheduled reparations. It got German industry going with large amounts of US cash and the economy got a big boost. Pensions and wages rose; more people got jobs. However, this made Germany dependent on America. There was still unemployment, the rich had to pay higher taxes and farmers' income fell. The **Young Plan (1929)** continued Stresemann's work of revising the Treaty of Versailles and especially the reparations. They were further reduced and rescheduled.

Stresemann died on 8 October 1929. Two weeks later the American stock market crashed.

Exam practice

This is an example of a Question 1a–c from Section A.

1. **a)** What do Sources A and B suggest about Weimar Germany? **(4 marks)**

Answers online   *Exam practice continues on page 98*

Exam practice continues on page 98

Exam tip

Question 1a

Try **not** to just copy the words of Source B that seem to answer the question. The question uses the word *'suggest'*. Try to use your own words that sum up the mood or main message of the source(s). This can often be the same as your first impression of the picture in Source A.

Source A: *A photograph of a German farming family in 1925*

Source B: *From a report by Sir John Sandelman Allen, the chairman of a group of seven British MPs who visited Germany for sixteen days in 1928*

'We are very impressed that industrialists show great confidence in the future and are spending money on new factories and the reconstruction of Germany. The workers put in long hours. Even in heavy populated areas of Germany there is little unemployment. There seems a general air of stability. The iron and steel works have plenty of orders …

There is little or no war spirit; instead a general determination to improve things. There is general acceptance that the Weimar Republic is essential for the future development of Germany.'

Revision task

Read the following list of Stresemann's policies and write a sentence to say whether it would have made his government popular or unpopular:
- Ended passive resistance and paid reparations
- New currency
- Trade link with Russia
- Joining League of Nations
- Dawes Plan

1. b) What different view of Weimar Germany is suggested by Sources C and D? *(6 marks)*

c) Why do you think Sources A and B give a different view to Sources C and D? *(8 marks)*

Source C: *A family are given free food in a Berlin Salvation Army soup kitchen in 1931*

Source D: *From a speech by Chancellor Franz von Papen commenting on Germany's situation in 1932*

'Germany's problems are the debts she owes, the heavy taxation of her people, high interest rates and above all unemployment. Unemployment is more widespread than in any other country and affects a quarter of the population. It uses up a lot of government money. However, what is particularly damaging is the ever-growing number of young people who have no possibility of finding employment and earning a living. As a result young people are desperate and turn to political extremism.'

Exam tip

Question 1b

In Question 1b, concentrate on Sources C and D to begin with. Follow the advice given for Question 1a. Try **not** to just copy the words of Source D that seem to answer the question. The question uses the word '*suggested*', so try to use your own words that sum up the mood or main message of the source. This can often be the same as your first impression of the picture in Source C. Finally say **how** the impression you get from Sources C and D is different from the impression in Sources A and B (page 97). The word '*whereas*' is useful to join the two impressions together in one sentence, '*In Sources C and D it seems like the workers are … whereas in Sources A and B the impression is that they …*' Do not try to explain **why** there is a difference – that belongs in your answer to Question 1c!

Question 1c

There are many things to look for when trying to explain **why** different people at different times have different views about history. One of the simplest ways to start examining different views and sources is to use the **TAP** idea. TAP stands for **T**ime, **A**uthor and **P**lace.

T **Time**
A **Author**
P **Place**

Think about each aspect in turn in your answer and try to connect it with the history you have learned.

- **Time**: are the sources from different times in history? What knowledge do you have about the events at that time that might help explain what the sources say or show?

- **Author**: are the authors different? What do you know about the author or artist or photographer that might help you explain the view they have or the image they have produced? Who is the audience?

- **Place**: are the sources from or about different places? What do you know or can guess at that might explain why the difference in place might affect what is said, written or shown in the source?

3.2 The Nazi rise to power 2: How was Hitler able to come to power?

On 8–9 November 1923 Hitler and the Nazis tried to start a revolution in Germany by taking over the government in southern Germany (the Munich Putsch). They failed. However, Hitler learned some important political lessons from the event and by 1933 had become the German Chancellor.

Key content

- The Munich Putsch and the Nazi Party
- The origins and organisation of the Nazi Party after 1920
- How the Depression affected Germany
- How Hitler and the Nazis took advantage of the Depression
- How Hitler became Chancellor in 1933

The Munich Putsch and the Nazi Party

Revised ☐

What did Hitler learn from the Munich Putsch?

1. Hitler would use democratic methods to get power through elections.

2. He would redesign the Nazi Party to increase its appeal to voters.

Revision task

Study the table on page 95 in section 3.1. Rearrange the following statements in the correct order to remind you of what happened in the Munich Putsch, 1923.

- They agreed to set up a separate government in Bavaria.
- Hitler was arrested two days later.
- Hitler and the Nazis marched into the centre of Munich.
- Kahr spoke at a political meeting in a beer hall.
- Hitler was sent to prison.

- The police stopped the march.
- Hitler escaped the firing.
- Hitler interrupted Kahr, the leader of Bavaria.
- Hitler was put on trial.
- In prison Hitler wrote his book, *Mein Kampf*.
- The police opened fire on the marchers.
- Hitler held Kahr prisoner in the beer hall.

Key person

Adolf Hitler

- Adolf Hitler was born in 1889 in Austria.
- He wanted to become an artist but was rejected by art school.
- He fought on the Western Front in the First World War and was wounded twice, temporarily blinded by poison gas and decorated for bravery.
- When he left the army he joined a small German political party. Hitler made a big impact with his public speaking and soon he was in control.

- He led an unsuccessful putsch in November 1923 for which he served nine months in prison.
- While in prison, Hitler wrote a book, *Mein Kampf* (My Struggle). In it he explained what he thought had gone wrong with Germany and how it could be put right in the future.

The origins and organisation of the Nazi Party after 1920

Revised

The National Socialist German Workers Party or the Nazi Party was formed in 1920.

- The Nazi Party began using a new symbol (the **swastika**), a new flag and the raised right arm salute.

- It published its new 25-point manifesto or programme. Hitler took a new title – **Der Führer** – meaning 'Leader'.

- He created the first 'strong arm' squads made up mainly of former soldiers or **Freikorps**. These were the core of the **Sturmabteilung** (SA), or storm troopers. They would be the muscle of the new party, guarding their own meetings and disrupting those of others.

- Hitler bought a weekly newspaper – *Völkischer Beobachter* (the People's Observer) – in which to promote their ideas.

- The first mass meetings were advertised and held. Party members were given training in public speaking. They concentrated their message on the middle classes and farmers. They had less success with the workers, but membership of the Nazi Party grew steadily.

- Following the Munich Putsch in 1925, Hitler built up the party and created regional party bosses who answered to Hitler alone.

- He encouraged Nazi associated groups to form for doctors, students, teachers and other professions.

How the Depression affected Germany

Revised

The Depression made the German people poor

- After the First World War under the Dawes Plan (1924) the American government and banks gave money to Germany to pay for the reconstruction of the country.

- In October 1929 the price of shares in American companies dropped to rock bottom on the US stock market on Wall Street, New York. American investors had suddenly lost all confidence in the value of the shares. They wanted their money back. One after another sold their shares and as a result, the prices fell. It became known as the **Wall Street Crash**.

- The Wall Street Crash affected Germany because after the First World War Germany's economy had been rebuilt with American money. Now the US banks wanted their money back.

- Germany could not give the money back as it had been used to set up factories. At the same time, throughout the world, demand fell for the goods that factories produced. German factories closed and workers lost their jobs.

The German people became disillusioned with the Weimar government

- In Germany there were 6 million people out of work in 1932. The government needed to find money to give to the poor to help them. But because so many people were out of work the government had less money coming in from taxes.

- Chancellor **Brüning** tried to get more money in by raising taxes and paying less money out by cutting the benefits of the unemployed. This made him and the government unpopular with everyone – those in, and out, of work. The President, **Hindenburg**, backed his Chancellor and pushed through the cuts with the power of Article 48.

- Things did not get better. Brüning helped the farmers – he put taxes on foreign food which just made German food expensive for everyone. Brüning was known as the 'Hunger Chancellor'.

- There was growing support for extreme parties like the Nazis and the Communists.

Revision task

Read how the Depression affected Germany. Copy and complete the following table by noting how the Depression affected individual Germans economically.

	How were people affected during the Depression?
Jobs	
Unemployment pay	
Wages	
Food prices in shops	
Taxes	

How Hitler and the Nazis took advantage of the Depression

Revised

The German people became desperate for solutions to their problems and the Nazis exploited the situation. Several things helped the Nazis do this.

Propaganda

Organised by **Josef Goebbels**, the Nazis were able to spread their message more effectively than other political parties.

- They used the latest technology such as loudspeakers and film.
- They staged big rallies to demonstrate their power and give a sense of discipline and order.
- They created posters with simple slogans that were memorable.
- Hitler used cars and planes to fly around Germany giving speeches.

Hitler's leadership

Hitler was an inspiring public speaker. He was able to sense what his audience wanted to hear and deliver powerful and convincing speeches.

- He offered simple solutions to complex problems.
- Hitler chose topics that would get an emotional response from a lot of Germans. He spoke about the shame of the Treaty of Versailles; he played on fears about communism; he criticised the Weimar government as weak and run by Jews.

Nazi promises

The Nazis made a number of key promises to attract voters.

- Hitler promised to solve Germany's economic problems.
- He said he would build up the army and make Germany great again.
- He blamed the Jews for a lot of Germany's problems and said that he wanted to build a pure Germany that would expand its borders to the east.
- Hitler's opposition to communism brought the Nazi Party money from businessmen to pay for its election campaigns.

Weimar weaknesses

- The Weimar government struggled to deal with the economic problems. They appeared weak and divided.

- As the Social Democrats and the Communist Party did not get on with each other there was not a united response to Hitler.

- The Nazis by way of contrast seemed decisive and confident. When more people voted for them the Social Democrats became scared and supported Brüning's harsh measures to control Weimar government spending, pay and prices.

- As a result, the German people became disillusioned with traditional parties and politicians.

- By 1929 the Nazis were well organised and had over 100,00 members. Local leaders who had been trained in public speaking ran public meetings. The Hitler Youth attracted the support of young people. Local Nazi Party groups helped the unemployed with soup kitchens, shelters or action in the SA.

Violence

- The Nazis became even more violent and provocative between 1930 and 1932. They marched in the streets, beat up opponents and disrupted meetings. The Nazis appeared powerful and disciplined.

- It appeared as if the Weimar government could not keep control.

- They disrupted German life so much that Brüning decided to ban the Nazis. This led to a political deal between a few key people that brought Hitler into power.

Revision task

Copy and complete the table below by explaining how each of the factors would have encouraged Germans to vote for the Nazis.

Factor	Impact on or appeal to voters
Propaganda	
Leadership	
Nazi promises	
Weimar weaknesses	
Violence	

Key people

- **Paul von Hindenburg (1847–1934)** was an experienced general and field marshal. Retired 1918. Elected president in 1925 and again in 1932. His authority guaranteed the governments of Brüning, Schleicher and von Papen who ruled by presidential decree. Died in office.

- **Heinrich Brüning (1885–1970)** was Weimar Chancellor. A Christian trade union official who was elected to the Reichstag for the Centre Party. Ruled by presidential decree from 1930 to 1932.

- **Kurt von Schleicher (1882–1934)** was General and last Chancellor of Weimar.

- **Franz von Papen (1879–1969)** was German Chancellor (1932).

How Hitler became Chancellor in 1933
Revised

1. Brüning banned the Nazi SA on 13 April 1932. **General Kurt von Schleicher**, head of the German army, thought that this was unwise. The Nazi SA opposed the Communists on the streets and counter-balanced the Communist threat. He persuaded President Hindenburg not to support Brüning's ban and without presidential backing Brüning could not govern so he resigned (30 May 1932). Schleicher's man to replace Brüning was **von Papen**. Schleicher arranged Nazi support for von Papen's government with the promise of a new set of elections and no banning of the SA.

2. When the promised election came in July 1932, the Nazis polled the largest ever vote in the history of Reichstag elections. They became the largest party in the Reichstag with 230 seats. However, this did not give them the majority they needed to control the Reichstag. Hitler and the Nazis celebrated their success with an outbreak of violence against their opponents. Hitler demanded the job of Chancellor but Hindenburg refused.

3. Von Papen realised that he would not get any support from the Nazis, so he called new elections. The Nazi vote in the November elections of 1932 fell a little. Von Papen wanted to make big changes to the Weimar Constitution so that it would be easier for him to rule Germany. General Schleicher thought this a bad move. He persuaded

Hindenburg to sack von Papen and make himself Chancellor. Von Papen was furious.

4. Von Papen plotted his return to power. He wanted to use the popularity of Hitler and the Nazis but control the amount of real power that they had. So on 4 January 1933 he 'bought' Nazi support in a secret meeting with Hitler. Von Papen offered Hitler the job of Chancellor and one other government job for a Nazi. Hitler, alarmed by the slight fall in support for the Nazis in November 1932, agreed. General Schleicher did not run the government well and he was sacked by President Hindenburg. Hitler became Chancellor on 30 January 1933.

Revision task

To understand the political deal that gave Hitler the job of Chancellor you have to understand the roles of President Hindenburg, General Schleicher and von Papen. Place the following events in order on a timeline like this.

April 1932   January 1933
├───┼───┼───┼───┼───┼───┼───┼───┼───┼───┤

Events

Secret meeting of Hitler and von Papen	Brüning bans the SA
Von Papen becomes Chancellor	Von Papen plans to change the Weimar Constitution
Nazis become largest party in Reichstag	General Schleicher appointed Chancellor
Von Papen sacked	Brüning resigns
Hitler becomes Chancellor	Nazis lose 34 Reichstag seats in election
Hitler demands the job of Chancellor	General Schleicher sacked

Exam practice

This is an example of a Question 2c or 3c from Section B.

'It was the Depression that enabled Hitler to become Chancellor of Germany in 1933.' How far do you agree with this interpretation of how important the Depression was in bringing Hitler and the Nazis to power in 1933? Explain your answer.   **(12 marks)**
SPaG: (4 marks)

Answers online

Exam tip

This type of question is called an **iceberg question** because the interpretation (the statement) highlights **the Depression** as a factor but excludes the other factors.

However, the question is really about **all** the factors which explain why Hitler was able to become Chancellor in 1933. Other interpretations could be put forward which focus on the other factors – they are the part of the iceberg below the water.

The best answers will have several short paragraphs, each of which explains a different factor. In the conclusion you should answer the question: in the light of these other factors, how convinced are you by this interpretation?

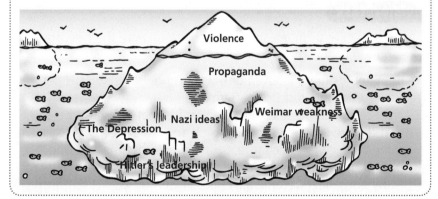

3.3 Control and opposition 1: How did Hitler create a dictatorship?

Hitler became Chancellor on 30 January 1933 but he had limited power and still needed the Reichstag to pass laws. Von Papen was determined to keep the Nazis under control so Hitler was only allowed to appoint one Nazi minister. He picked the Minister of the Interior (Head of the Police) and appointed Wilhelm Frick. Violence and tension between Nazis and Communists grew before the elections planned for March 1933.

Key content

- The Reichstag Fire, 1933
- How Hitler completed the takeover of the government

The Reichstag Fire, 1933

Revised

On 27 February 1933 the German parliament building, the Reichstag, was burned down by a solitary, former Communist, Marinus van der Lubbe. **The Reichstag Fire** was an opportunity the Nazis seized. They could gain more power and discredit the Communists.

- After the fire Hitler acted quickly. He persuaded President Hindenburg that a Communist plot existed. He signed the **Decree for the Protection of the People and the State** which gave Hitler special powers. Hitler could lock up his Communist opponents, ban their newspapers and give his SA storm troopers police powers, which they enjoyed using, to attack Communists. Hitler had the 81 Communist members of the Reichstag arrested.
- Businessmen, frightened by the Communist menace, backed the Nazis with cash to fight the election.
- In the 3 March 1933 elections, Hitler's Nazi Party won 288 seats. He then banned the Communist Party (KPD) which gave him a Reichstag majority.
- Hitler wanted total power and needed two-thirds of the Reichstag to back him. The Catholic Centre Party were reassured by Hitler's promises to protect the Catholic Church in Germany and so supported the Nazis.
- The **Enabling Act** was passed on **23 March 1933** which allowed Hitler to pass any law he liked without Reichstag permission. The Reichstag had just voted itself out of existence!

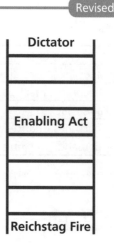

Dictator

Enabling Act

Reichstag Fire

Revision task

The two key events in making Hitler a dictator were the Reichstag Fire and the Enabling Act.

1. Copy the diagram (above/right) which shows the steps Hitler took to become dictator in Germany.
2. Now complete the first three blank steps that show the ways that the fire led to the Enabling Act. You should be able to find three things which meant that Hitler would get the Enabling Act passed by the Reichstag. You can add another two steps later to show how Hitler became a dictator in Germany.
3. Add your own notes to your steps in different colours for actions that show fears, luck, political cleverness, and ruthlessness.
4. Add notes for the two further steps in the diagram that show how Hitler became dictator.

Exam practice

This is an example of a Question 2c or 3c from Section B.

'It was the Reichstag Fire that enabled Hitler to become dictator of Germany after 1933.' How far do you agree with this interpretation of how Hitler became dictator after 1933? Explain your answer.
(12 marks)
SPaG: **(4 marks)**

Answers online

After the Enabling Act the Nazis set about bringing into line – or 'Nazifying' (*Gleichschaltung*) – all organisations with power in Germany.

- Trade unions were merged into the Nazi labour organisation – DAF (2 May 1933).
- Political parties were banned or forced to disband. The Nazi Party became the only legal political party in Germany (14 July 1933).
- A Concordat (agreement) was signed with the Catholic Church stating that it would stay out of politics (8 July 1933).
- State governments were abolished and replaced with Nazi state governors.

How did Hitler become all-powerful within the Nazi Party?

After Hitler gained so much power in Germany he still had a problem within the Nazi Party itself. Hitler had appointed an old friend, Ernst Röhm, to lead the SA in 1930 and to control their violent behaviour. Once the SA had been a valuable political asset, but by 1934 Röhm and his 2 million men had become a serious embarrassment to Hitler. Hitler wanted to keep the support of big business and the army. Röhm's men seemed determined to upset Hitler's powerful supporters, especially the army which feared a takeover by the SA. So Hitler acted.

1. On 29 June 1934 Hitler acted to prevent what he called a 'second revolution' led by Röhm. Himmler's black-shirted Schutzstaffel (SS) organised the murders of Röhm and hundreds of SA leaders. SA leaders were dragged from their beds in the night, taken to Nazi headquarters and shot. Röhm too was arrested by Hitler. When he refused to commit suicide, he was shot in prison. This event became known as '**The Night of the Long Knives**'.

2. The remaining SA leaders learned the lesson and its new leadership did exactly what Hitler told them. They performed ceremonial duties and provided shows of force.

3. The army generals were pleased and when on 2 August 1934 President Hindenburg died, the President's power was merged with the Chancellor's. The army swore loyalty to Adolf Hitler who took a new title – Der Führer (the leader). Adolf Hitler now had total power in Germany.

Exam tip

It is common to have questions about how Hitler became the dictator of Germany. Remember the **iceberg question** (see page 103). The iceberg question puts forward one interpretation and asks you to evaluate it.

The question wants you to show that you understand how there can be several interpretations based on different events that explain how Hitler became dictator. This is how one such paragraph might read. We have highlighted it to show:

- the answer is showing knowledge of events
- the answer is explaining the impact of events
- linking to the next paragraph.

It was luck that the Reichstag burned down on 27 February 1933. Marinus van der Lubbe said he was acting alone but the fire was so destructive it was thought one man alone could not do so much damage. It was luck that the fire did do so much damage. The Nazis did not do it but they seized on it and exploited it quickly to create a mood of panic. It was bad luck for Hindenburg that he died, but fortunate for Hitler. He could become Führer. He could merge the jobs of Chancellor and President into one and get the army to swear their loyalty. Hitler obviously could not count on good luck but he could offer strong, decisive leadership.

Now write some paragraphs for each of the following interpretations to follow the one on the **Reichstag Fire**. In each paragraph say what the event was (two to three sentences) and what impact it had (two to three sentences). In your conclusion remember to comment on which event you think is the most convincing.

- Luck
- The Enabling Act
- The Night of the Long Knives
- Hitler's leadership

Key

Knowledge of events

Impact of event in making Hitler dictator

Linking to next paragraph

Control and opposition 2: How effectively did the Nazis control Germany, 1933–45?

3.4

3.4 Control and opposition 2: How effectively did the Nazis control Germany, 1933–45?

The Nazi state controlled Germans through terror. People who criticised the Nazi regime or their policies were at risk of imprisonment or torture by **the Gestapo** or secret police. Anyone suspected of opposition might be beaten up, lose their job or sent to a concentration camp. Even the courts were under Nazi control so any form of opposition was difficult to organise and dangerous to keep up.

Key content

● The nature of the totalitarian state

● Opposition to Hitler and the Nazis

● The reasons why more people did not resist and oppose the Nazis

The nature of the totalitarian state   Revised

The Nazis used a number of methods to make sure that they controlled how people behaved.

Informers

Every town had its **informers** who would keep the police informed about what went on and who said what. The Gestapo used this information to arrest anti-Nazis without a trial, then torture and imprison them in concentration camps.

The police

The police were controlled by the Nazis. The police collected information that could be used to try Germans in the '**People's Courts**' where all the judges had been appointed by the Nazis.

Concentration camps

Concentration camps were originally temporary prisons for Nazi opponents but they soon became **forced labour camps**. By the late 1930s the SS ran factories using slave labour from these camps.

The SS

The SS were originally Hitler's personal bodyguard but by 1939 had 240,000 members. They were **elite** Aryans who were fiercely loyal to Hitler.

The law

The number of offences carrying the death penalty went up from three in 1933 to 46 in 1943. These included listening to foreign radio stations, telling anti-Nazi jokes or having sexual relations with a Jew.

The media

The Nazis controlled what was written in newspapers or heard on the radio. Posters praised Hitler and explained what was expected of loyal Germans. Ordinary Germans were frightened to speak out and did not know who to trust.

Key term

Aryans – Nazi term for white, blond-haired, blue-eyed and physically fit Europeans. In practice, it became a Nazi term for non-Jewish Germans.

Opposition to Hitler and the Nazis

Political parties

- Opposition to the Nazis in the 1920s and early 1930s came from left-wing political parties – the **Communists** and the **Social Democrats**.
- In 1933 they had been banned. Both parties set up secret 'underground' organisations.
- **The Communists** were Hitler's declared enemies. Their spy rings collected information that would help the Soviet Union. The last ring was the Rote Kapelle (Red Orchestra), destroyed by the Gestapo in August 1943.
- **The Social Democrats (SPD)** tried to organise resistance among factory workers through propaganda leaflets, illegal newspapers and political meetings. Many members of the SPD fled from Germany in 1933. Their contacts within the country sent reports to their base in Prague until 1938 when they moved to Paris and then London (1941).
- Neither Social Democrats nor Communists co-operated with the other or achieved any serious resistance.

Key people

Martin Niemöller – Anti-Nazi Protestant priest. Leader of the Confessing Church. He was put in a concentration camp.

Dietrich Bonhoeffer – Protestant priest. Member of Confessing Church. Worked with anti-Nazi resistance. Arrested in 1943, he was killed in a concentration camp in 1945.

Christian resistance efforts

- Nearly all Germans were Christians – one-third were Catholic and two-thirds were Protestant. The Nazis used and kept the support of the Christian Church. Many Christians supported the Nazis. Christians who didn't were isolated.
- Paul Schneider was a priest who refused to stop preaching against the Nazis. He was put in a concentration camp in 1937 and beaten.
- Men like Martin Niemöller and Dietrich Bonhoeffer opposed Hitler.
- The Catholic Archbishop of Münster, Graf Clemens von Galen, spoke out bravely and successfully against the Nazis' **euthanasia** programme in 1941. Recognising his popularity the Nazis abandoned their programme.

Exam tip

Be aware of key dates when thinking about resistance and opposition. Questions often carry dates in them. The key dates are **1933** when Hitler came to power and **1934** when he was dictator. Opposition before 1933 is different to opposition after 1933, when Hitler was in power.

Student resistance

- With the retreat of the German armies from Russia in 1942, students at Munich University began producing anti-Nazi leaflets and graffiti. The ringleaders of **the White Rose Group** were Hans and Sophie Scholl, along with Christopher Probst, Alex Schmorell, Willi Graf and Professor Kurt Huber.
- They were upset by the apathy of the people in the face of Nazi actions. Hans Scholl had served as a medical orderly along with Schmorell and Graf on the Russian front. They knew of the atrocities that took place.
- The ringleaders were arrested in February 1943. Tried by a People's Court and condemned to death, they were guillotined.

Youth resistance

- Young people who disliked the Hitler Youth movements formed their own groups such as the **Edelweiss Pirates** or the **Swing Youth**.
- The Pirates were working-class youths who attacked Hitler Youth groups, sang anti-Hitler songs, went on their own camping trips and had no time for the discipline of the Hitler Youth. In 1942 some of their leaders were hanged in Düsseldorf.
- Swing Youth were inspired by English and American jazz culture, music and clothes. They admired the decadent culture of Germany's wartime enemies. Their meetings were broken up and banned. Their ringleaders had their hair cut and some were sent to concentration camps.

The Kreisau Circle

- In the 1940s there was resistance from Germans much closer to the centre of government. They were disturbed by the brutality of the Nazis and alarmed by the development of Hitler's plans for war. The '**Kreisau Circle**' were influential

Germans who talked of ridding Germany of Hitler and the Nazis but they did nothing.

- A meeting planned between one of them, Father Alfred Delp, and Professor Kurt Huber of the 'White Rose' did not take place because the Gestapo arrested Delp. The 'Kreisau Circle' were arrested and executed in 1944–45.

The Beck–Goerdeler Group

- A more substantial opposition group formed around the former army leader, General Ludwig Beck, who had resigned over Hitler's invasion of Austria in 1938, and Karl Goerdeler, a Nazi official replaced in 1936.

- From the time Hitler seemed to be moving towards war, many more highly placed Germans saw disaster ahead for Germany. They looked for help from those countries outside Germany who would also suffer if Hitler began another war.

- Britain was sceptical about the opposition and followed an appeasement policy in the 1930s. Britain kept contacts with opposition groups alive but at arm's length.

- The **Beck–Goerdeler Group** was willing to take decisive, violent action to remove Hitler. By 1942 they agreed that Hitler would have to be killed. There were two small-scale attempts in March and November 1943 and then the 'July Plot' in 1944.

The Stauffenberg July Bomb Plot

- On 20 July 1944 they planned and carried out an attempt to blow up Hitler at his 'wolf's lair' headquarters in East Prussia. Colonel Claus von Stauffenberg arrived with a bomb in his briefcase.

- At 12.42 an explosion shattered the room. But Hitler survived.

- Stauffenberg was arrested and shot by the Gestapo. Hitler took a savage revenge on all those involved. He had 5746 people executed. The failure of the plot brought the German army under the tight control of the SS.

> **Revision task**
>
> Draw up a table to compare all of the ways the groups on pages 107–108 resisted and opposed the Nazis.

The reasons why more people did not resist and oppose the Nazis

Revised

1. **Fear**: the Nazis used the concentration camp and the threat of it to make sure that people behaved. There was a network of informers in flats and at work who would tell the Gestapo if people spoke out against the Nazis. Random violence and the disappearance of people added to a climate of fear and suspicion.

2. **Isolation**: It was hard to know what to do or who to trust. Many of those who resisted did not know about other groups.

3. **Support for Nazi ideas**: many Germans disliked the Treaty of Versailles and liked the idea of Germany becoming strong again. Some may have held anti-Jewish views. Many were frightened of the Communists.

4. **No other political parties**: there was only one political party and no official way of voicing opposition.

5. **Propaganda**: the Nazis controlled the newspapers and the radio. They made sure that alternative views or criticisms were not heard.

6. **Self-interest**: it became very clear that to live a good life you had to follow the party line. Promotion and the best jobs depended on this. Nazi Party membership soared.

7. **Nazi successes**: many people thought the Nazis were delivering what they promised. Unemployment was falling and there was order and discipline on the streets.

8. **Lack of foreign support**: Britain talked to opposition groups but did not actively support them. Hitler was Germany's democratically elected leader, his replacement might be worse.

> **Exam practice**
>
> *This is an example of a Question 1e from Section A.*
>
> Why did Germans find it hard to resist and oppose the Nazis after 1933?
>
> **(10 marks) (AQA 2013)**
>
> **Answers online**

> **Exam tip**
>
> The best answers to this question will include five or six detailed reasons why the Germans did not oppose the Nazis and a conclusion that explains which of those were most important, and how the different reasons worked together.

3.5 German economy and society 1: How much change did the Nazis bring to German society?

The Nazis had clear ideas about how different groups would fit into society. German women and German workers would be expected to play their part in building the thousand-year Reich, or empire.

Key content

- What Nazis wanted from women
- How the lives of women changed under Nazi rule
- Nazis' success in getting what they wanted from women
- How Nazis weakened the influence of the Churches in Germany

What Nazis wanted from women

Revised ☐

- Nazi attitudes to women were traditional. They wanted women to **stay at home** and **have children**. This was summed up in the Nazi slogan of **Kinder, Küche und Kirche** ('Children, Kitchen and Church').
- **Nazi organisations for women** were created, like the NSF (National Socialist Womanhood) and the DFW (German Women's Enterprise). They sent out a message that a woman's place was in the home and organised courses on motherhood and household management.
- The Nazis discouraged women from wearing modern fashions and make-up. In 1935 a Bavarian hotel banned 'women with red nails and long trousers' and in the town of Erfurt, police stopped women smoking in public.

How the lives of women changed under Nazi rule

Revised ☐

Staying at home

The Nazis wanted women to give up paid work and return to the home.

- Between 1933 and 1936 married women were banned from the top professional jobs as doctors, lawyers and senior civil servants.
- From June 1933 interest-free loans of 600 Reich marks (about four months' average industrial wage) were available to young women who left their jobs to get married.
- Labour exchanges and employers were asked to give first choice of **jobs to men**.

Having children

Nazi propaganda praised women who stayed at home and had babies.

- On 12 August, the birthday of Hitler's own mother, mothers were awarded medals. 'The Mother Cross' (bronze, silver and gold) went to women who had more than four, six or eight children.
- After 1933 the Nazis **made abortion illegal**, restricted the availability of contraceptive advice and facilities, and greatly improved maternity benefits and family allowances.
- Women who could not have babies could be easily divorced.
- After 1935 Jewish women could not marry Aryan men. The Nazis operated maternity homes – the SS-run Lebensborn (Spring of Life) – to look after the orphaned or illegitimate children of racially sound Germans.

Revision task

Make your own copy of this diagram and add notes about the Nazis' policies towards women.

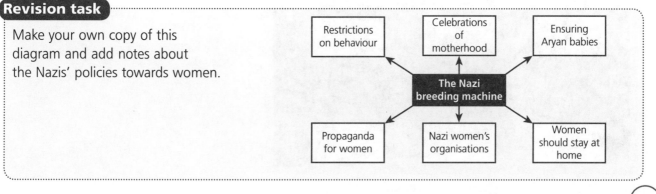

Nazis' success in getting what they wanted from women

- Hitler needed a large army to expand Germany's borders and build an empire. Unfortunately the population had been falling between 1930 and 1933. Nazis' policies were successful because the **population** grew at a faster rate. Between 1933 and 1939 the number of births over deaths increased from 233,297 to 558,891 which was an extra quarter of a million.

- The Nazis also wanted women to give up work and concentrate on the home. They had been elected partly because they promised to provide more jobs. Every job left by a woman returning to the home was available for a man. Between 1933 and 1937 the number of **women in the workforce fell** from 37 per cent to 31 per cent.

- A problem came when the Nazis prepared Germany for war. Women provided cheap and reliable labour and were too useful to the German economy to keep at home. The Nazis had to relax the restrictions on women working from 1938. There were practical reasons for having women in the workforce which went against the Nazis' theory of a woman's place being in the home.

Exam practice

This is an example of a Question 1d from Section A.

1. How useful is Source E for understanding family life under the Nazis?

   Explain your answer using Source E and your own knowledge.

   (8 marks) *(AQA 2008)*

Answers online

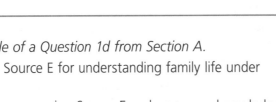

Source E: *A picture of an ideal German family in a painting called* Family *by Wolfgang Willrich, 1934*

Exam tip

The best answers will look at two aspects of the source:

1. What does the content of the source tell us about the family in Nazi Germany that makes it useful or not? The content of the source can be checked against your own knowledge of the topic.

2. What does the provenance of the source (who produced it, why it was produced, who it was produced for, where and when it was produced) tell us about how useful, or not, the source might be?

Don't forget that this question is about how useful the source is. You must say how useful the source is in your answer or you will lose marks. And remember to bring in your own knowledge too!

The Nazis viewed religion as a threat to their power and influence. Christian ideals threatened the acceptance of Nazism in society, but as Germany was such a religious country the Nazis dared not directly attack the Churches. What is more, German Catholics had consistently supported the Centre Party in politics.

The Nazis and the Roman Catholic Church

- Hitler came to an agreement, called a **Concordat**, with the Pope in Rome in July 1933.
- The Concordat offered religious freedoms of worship and education for German Catholics. In return the Catholic Church agreed to stay out of politics. The Centre Party was dissolved in July 1933.
- Hitler had no intention of keeping his promises to the Pope. From the start of 1934 Catholic priests were harassed and arrested, their schools interfered with and their youth clubs criticised.
- In 1937 Pope Pius XI made his disillusionment known in a famous statement, 'With Burning Anxiety', in which he attacked the Nazi system.
- Nazi persecution of priests continued after 1937; many were put in concentration camps.
- In August 1941 **Cardinal Archbishop Galen** bravely criticised the Nazis for their abuse of human rights and their euthanasia programme.

German Protestants and the Nazis

- The German Protestant Churches split into two groups.
- Some admired the Nazis and wanted to see their church under Nazi control. They were called 'German Christians' (*Deutsche Christen*). Their leader, Ludwig Müller, became the first Reich Bishop in September 1933.
- Changes like this angered other German Protestant ministers. They felt the conflict between Nazi ideas and the basic beliefs of Christianity. They were led by a strong critic of the Nazis Pastor Martin Niemöller.

- Niemöller started the 'Confessing Church' in October 1934. Its ministers kept their Protestant faith and continued to criticise the Nazi regime.
- Niemöller was sent to a concentration camp in July 1937 along with many other Confessing Church ministers. His church was banned.

The success of Nazi religious policy

- Hitler was successful in weakening the Churches as a source of resistance to his policies.
- A Ministry of Churches was established under the leadership of Hanns Kerrl.
- Church schools were abolished and Catholic youth clubs closed so young people had to go to the Hitler Youth.
- The Churches and the priests were criticised in Nazi newspapers. Many priests and ministers were arrested.
- The effect of Nazi policies varied from place to place. In some areas local Nazi leaders sent their SA men in to beat up priests, in others they went to church every Sunday and sang in the choir.
- However, persecution increased after 1940. Monasteries were closed, church property attacked and church activities further restricted.

Why did Hitler and the Nazis succeed in weakening the Christian Churches?

- Some senior Catholic churchmen **favoured** the Nazis because the Communists would abolish the Churches.
- The Protestant Church was **divided** and closely tied to the German state. It was not part of a worldwide organisation like the German Catholic Church.
- The Nazis were **too clever** to attempt attacking the Churches directly. The Nazis' policy was to wear the Churches down. They made it difficult for Christians to worship, but the churches remained open. This made it hard for the Church to fight back.

Revision tasks

1. Make a list of all the ways in which the Nazis influenced and controlled the Christian Churches in Germany.

2. Make a list of all the ways in which the Christian Churches in Germany resisted and opposed the Nazi influence.

3.6 German economy and society 2: How successful were the Nazis in rebuilding the German economy?

Hitler's aims for the economy were to:

- provide the weapons for **war** – a 'defence economy'
- become **self-sufficient** in raw materials (especially oil) and foods
- expand Germany's borders, **gaining land** and resources
- tackle unemployment in Germany, so he needed to provide **jobs**.

Germany's big problem was that the country was still buying more than it was making and selling abroad. Hitler had to tackle this to deliver his economic objectives. So he asked a respected banker, Hjalmar Schacht, to take charge.

Key content

- Hitler's economic plans before the war
- Economic advantages and disadvantages for Germans living under the Nazis
- The impact of the war on the German people

Hitler's economic plans before the war

Revised

What	When	Who	Why	How	Success	Weaknesses
The New Plan	1934	Hjalmar Schacht	Wanted to provide raw materials to make weapons and complete building projects like *autobahns* (motorways) without spending much money.	• Strict limits on imports of consumer products. • Raw materials paid for with German-made goods.	• By 1935 Germany sold a small amount more than it bought making a trade surplus. • Unemployment was falling. • Production had increased by nearly 50% since 1933. • Germany was able to rearm its forces.	Raw materials for rearmament were too expensive. Hitler refused to cut back. He wanted to rearm faster. Hitler sacked Schacht!
The Four Year Plan	1936–1940	Goering	To increase food production and achieve self-sufficiency in certain raw materials like oil, rubber and metals.	• Use of synthetic or *ersatz* substitutes. • Even fewer imports. • Produce more raw materials. • Control wages and prices. • Use slave labour.	• Planned production of aluminium, steel and explosives was nearly achieved.	Germany could only keep going for a short war. But Goering failed to supply enough oil. The controls of the plan continued after 1940.

Economic advantages and disadvantages for Germans living under the Nazis

Unemployed men

- Hitler passed laws in 1933 to build *autobahns*, housing and other public works projects. He insisted the work be done by hand, not machines. Local councils built more cheap flats to solve the housing shortage of the Depression years.
- In 1934 as Germany rearmed, employers were encouraged to take on more workers.
- The Nazis relaunched Weimar's Labour Service (*Arbietsdienst*) on 26 June 1935 and made it compulsory for all young men between 18 and 25 to do physical work for six months. Wages on these schemes were sometimes lower than unemployment pay. But for some it was a lifeline to feed and clothe their families.
- Unemployment figures also fell because the Jews were not counted, women were encouraged to leave full-time jobs and the army was growing in size.

> **Exam tip**
>
> It is difficult to decide if the Germans were better off, much the same, or worse off under the Nazis. The short answer is it depended who you were and when you were asked. Be prepared to give examples of how your study of different groups in German society might demonstrate this idea.

Workers

- The Nazis kept food prices below their 1928–29 levels. Under the Nazis the production of some foods increased, others fell. It was harder to find and afford fats like cooking oils and butter.
- The average industrial worker's **pay stayed the same** from 1929 to 1938; however, the average **working week lengthened** from 43 hours in 1933 to 47 hours in 1939.
- Pay levels varied. In some industries – for example, arms making – wages went up; in others – for example, consumer goods production – wages went down.
- Workers had no trade unions to bargain for better conditions or higher wages. Trade unions were replaced by **DAF** which aimed to increase production rather than look after the workers. It ran the 'Strength through Joy' (KdF) campaign which appealed to workers by offering free holidays, trips to concerts or sporting events. They were even offered the chance to save five marks a week for a Volkswagen car, none of which were ever delivered.

Owners of small businesses

- Some of the middle class did not prosper under the Nazis. The small businesses upon which they were dependent were squeezed out by big businesses. Small shopkeepers faced competition from large stores. By 1943, 250,000 retail businesses closed down.
- Many small businesses could not compete with the wages offered by large companies.
- The Nazis passed laws to ban new department stores and stop existing ones growing.
- Jewish businesses were closed down.
- Between 1936 and 1939 the number of self-employed craftsmen fell from 1.65 million to 1.5 million, but the value of their trade nearly doubled between 1933 and 1937.

Farmers

- Older farmers were upset that the Nazis kept **food prices fixed** below their 1928–29 levels. They remembered getting better prices in the 1920s. From 1937 farmers became poorer.
- The Nazis set quotas for the food each farm should produce. Farmers resented this official interference.
- Farmers suffered a labour shortage as workers left for better paid jobs in the factories and towns.
- The Nazis passed laws to protect the rights of farmers to own their farms.

Big business owners and industrialists

- Big businesses did well because they could help with rearmament and benefited most from the reduced power of the trade unions.
- Big businesses made **huge profits** if they produced what the Nazis wanted. The Nazis controlled prices, wages, profits and the supply of raw materials. The Nazis could supply a vast slave labour force.
- IG Farben became the biggest chemical company in Europe with Nazi help and doubled its profits between 1936 and 1940.

Working women

- **Unemployment figures fell** because women were encouraged to leave full-time jobs. By 1937 there were 6 per cent fewer women in work than in 1933.
- At the time many younger women resented the lack of opportunity as jobs were given to men.
- From 1938 this trend reversed and women went back to work; there were 3 million more women in work by September 1939.

Copy and complete the table below with one reason that each person might like or dislike what the Nazis did. Make sure you can explain your reasoning.

	Action by Nazis that they approved of	Action by Nazis that they disapproved of
Unemployed		
Workers		
Owners of small businesses		
Farmers		
Big business owners and industrialists		
Working women		

Exam practice

This is an example of a Question 2b or 3b from Section B.

1. Using Source F and your own knowledge, explain how the Nazis changed workers' lives. **(8 marks)**

Answers online

Source F: *Strength through Joy (KdF) poster produced in 1938. The caption reads, 'Save five marks a week if you want to drive your own car'*

The impact of the war on the German people

Hitler and the Nazis were in power for twelve and a half years. For six of those years Germany was at war. How did it affect German civilians?

Phase of the war	The effect on German civilians
Blitzkreig: Germany enjoyed military success from September 1939 to June 1941, described as a 'lightning war'. Germany invaded Poland and occupied most of western Europe.	● Rationing was introduced but it was fair and adequate. Germany took food from the land it conquered. ● Some bombing raids on cities but German defences were strong and the RAF attacked mainly military targets.
Operation Barbarossa: in June 1941, Hitler invaded Russia. The German war economy was not capable of supplying enough men and weapons for a long war. It was the beginning of the end.	● Clothing became scarce and rationed. Meat rations were down from 500 gm a week to 300 gm. ● Allies started the 'thousand bomber raids' of explosives and firebombs on towns and cities. ● There was a shortage of doctors to treat the wounded. ● Younger men were required to join the army to replace those killed, in turn more women were needed in factories. Slave labour was also used in factories.
Total War: February 1943–July 1945. Germany was defeated at Stalingrad. After the Battle of Kursk in the summer of 1943 the German armies were always retreating.	● Heavy bombing of the cities caused much death and homelessness. Water supplies were cut off along with electricity and telephones. ● Clothes supplies ended, much food was unavailable, transport and distribution were affected. ● Women were required to work in factories. ● Propaganda reinforced the idea of victory through the people's sacrifices.
Defeat: by July 1944 it was clear Germany would lose the war. Allied forces had landed on D-Day in June 1944 and fought their way towards Germany.	● Heavy air raids killed thousands. In Dresden on two nights in February 1945 nearly 150,000 people were killed. ● People scavenged for food. Ration system broke down. ● As Russian armies advanced in the East, millions became refugees and tried to get to the West.

Exam practice

This is an example of a Question 2b or 3b from Section B.

2.b) Using Source G and your own knowledge explain how the war affected German civilians. **(8 marks)**

Answers online

Source G: *Clearing up bomb damage in Berlin, 1944*

3.7 Youth and race 1: How successful were the Nazis in influencing young people?

The Nazis believed that to control Germany's future they had to make all young people loyal Nazis. They tried to do this through their schools and youth movements, shaping the minds of young Germans.

> **Key content**
> - Hitler Youth
> - The Nazis and education
> - The success of Nazi policies towards young people

Hitler Youth

Revised ☐

- Hitler Youth (HJ) organisations **indoctrinated** young people with important Nazi ideas and values – duty, obedience, honour, courage, strength and ruthlessness.
- Boys were taught **military-style** activities and the girls prepared for **motherhood**.
- Both girls and boys were expected to take part in appropriate **physical training**.

Young people were attracted by the exciting **outdoor activities**, for example, camping and hiking as well as sports. Some enjoyed the military aspects of the youth movements – the uniforms, the marching and the discipline. There was great comradeship among the Hitler Youth and always **competition** to do better or be the best. Using the young people in Hitler Youth organisations was a valuable way of spying on parents and teachers to make sure they supported the Nazis. The Nazi youth organisations formed another point of focus in the lives of many young Germans when they were not at school or at home.

> **Key people**
> - **Baldur von Schirach** – Leader of the Hitler Youth. Appointed 'Youth Leader of the Reich'.
> - **Bernhard Rust** – Reich Minister for Science and Education.

The Hitler Youth Laws

- **1936**: first Hitler Youth Law gave the HJ **equal status** to home and school. The law made it virtually impossible to avoid joining the Hitler Youth organisation. Some young people signed up but were not enthusiastic or regular members.
- **1939**: second Hitler Youth Law made membership of the Hitler Youth **compulsory**.

Nazi youth organisations

Age	Boys	Girls
10	DJ – German Young People	JM – League of Young Girls
14	HJ – Hitler Youth	BDM – League of German Girls
18	Army	Faith and Beauty (for ages 17–21, founded in 1938)

The Nazis and education

Revised ☐

The Nazis used the schools as well as the Nazi Youth movements to produce good young Nazis. The Nazis made changes that affected the teachers, the subjects taught and the schools themselves.

The Nazis and teachers

- The teachers were persuaded by a mixture of propaganda and threat into joining the **National Socialist Teachers' League** (NSLB). In January 1933 it had 6000 members; by 1937 this had grown to 320,000, or 97 per cent of the teaching profession.
- In their speeches, Hitler and leading Nazis showed that they had little respect for teachers.
- Teachers' work was increasingly interfered with by the Hitler Youth.
- Teachers who wanted jobs or promotion had to be given a reference saying that they were good Nazis.
- The teachers resented the crude Nazi propaganda produced for them and their students.

The Nazi curriculum

The Nazis took control of the school curriculum in all German schools. German, History, Biology and Physical Education were the most important school subjects for the Nazis.

- **German** literature studied was carefully chosen to show examples of German military success.
- **History** was given a special place in the curriculum so that children learned about the greatness of the German nation.
- **Biology** was used to teach children about Nazi ideas on race. Lessons explained the importance of making a racially sound marriage and the need to have children.
- **Physical Education** was essential for girls who would be the future mothers of the German nation. Boys needed to be fit in order to fight in the army. Students, therefore, had at least five hours a week of Physical Education such as gymnastics and athletics.
- Those with physical handicaps were refused a secondary education.

New Nazi schools

- In 1934 the Nazis set up the elite *Napolas* run by the SS and designed to provide the Nazi leaders of the future.
- Schirach and the Hitler Youth set up ten of their own elite 'Adolf Hitler Schools' in 1937.

Revision task

Write a paragraph about how the Nazis changed education. Write two or three sentences about the teachers, the curriculum and the new schools that were set up. Say how each aspect would change or influence young people.

The success of Nazi policies towards young people

Revised

- Most young people who joined the Hitler Youth movements in the 1930s enjoyed the activities and excitement of being part of the new movement.
- However, for some of those young people who joined the HJ after the start of the Second World War in 1939, and after the first youth leaders had joined the army, the compulsory physical activities, drill and obedience were disliked.

- The Nazis had to pass a second law in 1939 to force more young people to join the HJ.
- Many young people resented the discipline and having to spy on their friends and family.
- Some young people in the late 1930s rejected Nazi ideas and rebelled (see section 3.4, page 107).

Exam practice

These are examples of a Question 2a and 2b in Section B.

1. Why were young people important to the Nazis? **(4 marks)**
2. Use Source F and your own knowledge to explain how the Nazis tried to influence young people. **(8 marks)**

(AQA 2009)

Answers online

Source F: *An illustration from a Nazi children's school book*

Exam tip

The source will give you one thing to write about when answering a Question 2b. In this case it would be the way the Nazis wanted children to treat Jews and the use of illustrations in school textbooks to do that. To get a high mark you will need to use your own knowledge to write about and explain at least two other aspects that are relevant to the question. In this example you could also write about the Hitler Youth movements, rallies, what the children were taught, the laws against Jewish students in 1934 and the banning of Jewish children from schools in 1938.

3.8 Youth and race 2: How important in Germany were Nazi ideas on race?

Hitler saw a person's race as the key to their purpose and destiny. He thought all human history proved this. The perfect or master race was the **Aryan**; they were **superior**. Hitler wanted to create a racially pure Germany. He wanted to get rid of ethnic or religious minorities – such as Jews, gypsies and Slavs – that were regarded by the Nazis as **inferior**. They would be isolated, removed from positions of power and eventually eliminated. Hitler considered other groups to be impure or dangerous to the Aryan future he planned for Germany. For this reason

the physically or mentally disabled, homosexuals, criminals, alcoholics, the homeless and Jehovah's Witnesses were all persecuted.

> **Key content**
> - The Nazis and the Jews
> - What happened to the Jews when the Nazis took over?
> - Why Hitler was able to persecute the Jews

The Nazis and the Jews

Revised

Why did Hitler persecute the Jews?

- There was a long **tradition** in Europe of hostility towards the Jews which may be traced back to their treatment of Jesus.
- The Jews had a **distinctive** culture and were easily identifiable in most German towns.

- Jews often had a **'privileged'** position as doctors, lawyers or businessmen.
- Hitler personally hated the Jews from his time in Vienna as an art student. He blamed the Jews for all that was wrong with the world, and his own failures.

What happened to the Jews when the Nazis took over?

Revised

From 1933 Hitler persecuted the Jews and other minority groups. **Anti-Semitism** became government policy. Hitler did not set out to eliminate all Jews. The process happened **gradually**, each step making it easier for the next. At the start the Nazis wanted to remove all the Jews from Germany. This became more difficult as territory was won by the German army on the eastern front. The Nazis moved on to eliminate large numbers of Jews amongst the Russians they conquered.

> **Key term**
>
> **Anti-Semitism** – prejudice against and persecution of the Jews.

1933–36

- On 1 April 1933 Hitler ordered a boycott of Jewish shops, doctors, lecturers and lawyers.
- By May 1935 Jews were forbidden to join the army or have a government job.
- On 15 September 1935 the Nuremberg Laws prohibited marriage between Jews and non-Jews.

Any sexual relations between Jews and non-Jews outside marriage were criminal offences. Jews could not vote.

- During August 1936 Nazi anti-Semitism was relaxed as the world's press visited Germany for the Olympic Games.

1937–38

- From 1 March 1938 government contracts could not be awarded to Jewish firms.
- From 30 September only Aryan doctors were allowed to treat Aryan patients.
- On 7–8 November 1938 there was an attack on Jewish property, shops, homes and synagogues in all parts of Germany. Known as Kristallnacht (or 'Night of Broken Glass') about 100 Jews were killed and 20,000 sent to concentration camps. After **Kristallnacht** no one in Germany could be mistaken about the Nazis' policy towards the Jews.
- On 15 November 1938 Jewish schoolchildren were banned from ordinary German schools and had to attend Jewish schools.

1939–41

- On 1 September 1939 German Jews were subject to a curfew.

- The Nazis experimented with segregated areas for Jews called **ghettos** in the cities of Poland, with Warsaw as the largest. Many Jews died from starvation in the ghettos. The Nazis organised labour camps close to the ghettos.

- When the Second World War started Nazi treatment of Jews became harsher as the Nazis no longer cared about world opinion.

- With the invasion of Russia, on 22 June 1941, *Einsatzgruppen* (Action Squads) moved into Russia behind the advancing German armies to round up and kill Jews and Communists.

It is thought that they murdered 2.2 million Russians and Jews.

1941–45

- On 20 January 1942 Reinhard Heydrich summoned senior officials to Wannsee, Berlin to discuss the Jewish 'problem'. They decided how best to co-ordinate the plan for the 'Final Solution' which was Hitler's plan to exterminate all the Jews in German territory.

- The first extermination camp was built and began operating on 17 March 1942 at Belzec on the eastern Polish border.

- During 1943 many other camps in Poland, Germany and Austria were built.

Revision tasks

1. Read the three Nazi actions against the Jews in the table below. Complete the table by writing in two examples for each action.

Prevented the Jews from earning a living	Removed the rights of the Jews as citizens	Made violent attacks on the Jews

2. Explain why each of the following events in the table below marked a change in the Nazis' treatment of the Jews.

Event	Importance
The Nuremberg Laws, 1935	
Kristallnacht, 1938	
The start of the Second World War, 1939	
The invasion of Russia, 1941	
The Wannsee Conference, 1942	

3. Which event marked the biggest change in the Nazis' treatment of the Jews? Explain your answer.

Why Hitler was able to persecute the Jews

Revised

1. There was little German opposition to Nazi persecution of the Jews because Hitler had been so effective in **removing all opposition** within Germany and placing Nazis in positions of power.

2. Germans were subjected to a constant barrage of anti-Semitic **propaganda**. Some believed it. The German people were simply not told about some of the things that happened.

3. For many ordinary Germans who **felt powerless** to resist the persecution of Jews, they consoled themselves with the thought that this was the price they had to pay for all the other 'benefits' of Hitler's rule.

4. Some of those Nazis doing the killing were psychologically disturbed and enjoyed the work. Others believed they were merely being organised and efficient in the way they followed orders and dealt with a problem.

Exam tip

You don't have to remember everything that happened to the Jews. It is good if you can remember some examples of what happened to them to damage them financially, to take away their rights and then to hurt them physically. The **Revision task** above will help you with this. The five events in the table accompanying question 2 are important to remember. Work out a way of doing that.

3.9 Culture and propaganda: How did the Nazis change the cultural climate of Weimar Germany?

Under Nazi rule, cultural activities like art, music, theatre, literature, radio and film all had to show Nazi ideas. They would be anti-Semitic and glorify war. The arts put forward ideas of German nationalism, Aryan superiority, the cult of the Führer and a rejection of Christian values.

Key content

- The influence of the Nazis on culture
- The success of Nazi propaganda

The influence of the Nazis on culture

Revised

Weimar Germany		Nazi Germany
• Showed everyday life. • The Bauhaus movement was centred on Berlin. It tried to combine the arts and crafts in simple, elegant, modern, functional design. • Artists such as Kandinsky, Schlemmer and Klee came from this movement.	← ART →	• Painting and sculpture could not be abstract or modern. The Bauhaus was closed down by the Nazis after 1933. • German art had to be 'true to life' and clearly understandable by ordinary people. • In 1936 the Nazis publicly burnt 5000 paintings they disapproved of.
• A golden age for German cinema. • Modern technical methods used for horror and science fiction films, e.g. Fritz Lang's *Metropolis* (1927).	← CINEMA →	• Goebbels realised the growing popularity of film. • Nazi sympathisers like Alfred Hugenberg owned the studios. The work of some Germans, such as film director Leni **Riefenstahl**, is still praised today. All scripts were checked by the Propaganda Ministry. • The Nazis used film to record large set-piece Nazi political events for propaganda.
• Bauhaus architects used new technology to produce simple, pleasing shapes that were economical.	← ARCHITECTURE →	• The Nazis built on a grand scale, as in Ancient Rome, to inspire and celebrate victories. • The Nazi buildings linked to the past and stressed the importance of the community over the individual.
• Plays were set in the 1920s. • The aim was to shock and question established views. Brecht's *The Threepenny Opera* (1928) was a big hit and challenged traditional views of property ownership. It had a jazz-influenced score by Kurt Weill.	← THEATRE →	• Only traditional plays like those of Schiller, Goethe and Shakespeare were performed. • The **'Militant League for German Culture'** organised protests against 'modern' art. They protested against *The Threepenny Opera*, and the anti-war film *All Quiet on the Western Front* (1930).

	CABARET		Berlin's cabaret clubs were shut by the Nazis in 1933.
There was a liberated nightlife and more nakedness. Sex was discussed openly. Homosexuality was not frowned upon.	← CABARET →		• Berlin's cabaret clubs were shut by the Nazis in 1933.
• Novels often presented a bleak view of the world, e.g. Erich Remarque's description of German soldiers' experiences in *All Quiet on the Western Front* (1929) and Thomas Mann's *Magic Mountain* (1924).	← LITERATURE →		• There was strict censorship. Many German writers like Thomas Mann and Berthold Brecht left Germany. • In 1933 the Nazis raided libraries and publicly burned the books of authors who were not approved.
• Modern composers like Kurt Weill and Arnold Schoenberg who wrote contemporary classical music during the Weimar period were Jewish.	← MUSIC →		• Performances of classical music by Jewish composers like Mahler and Mendelssohn were banned. • Jazz music was criticised as 'Negroid', inferior and 'decadent'. • German music had to be patriotic, martial and popular.
• Physical exercise that was popular in the nineteenth century continued but individual sports like gymnastics gave way to competitive team sports like football. • Sports were strongly influenced by America, e.g. boxing became popular.	← SPORT →		• Sports and physical exercise were a major part of the Hitler Youth activities. • The Nazis used the 1936 Olympic Games for propaganda. Leni Riefenstahl made a film of the Games. • During the Games there was some reduction in anti-Semitism. • The Nazis were disappointed by the success of the black American athlete, Jesse Owens, who won four gold medals.

Revision task

Each of the following statements has one deliberate mistake and one missing word. Write out the sentences, correct the mistake and add the missing word from those below.

> black   Bauhaus   culture   Mahler   Mann   *Metropolis*
> cabaret   Brecht

- The Nazis opened _____ clubs in Berlin in 1933.
- Fritz Lang's _____ was a good example of a Weimar science fiction book.
- The _____ athlete, Jesse Owens, won six gold medals in the 1936 Olympics.
- The *Magic Mushroom* (1924) was a book by the German novelist, Thomas _____.
- The _____ was a design school that was closed down by the Nazis in 1930.
- The Militant League of German _____ was a Nazi group that protested against traditional art.
- Jewish composers like _____ were popular in Nazi Germany.
- *The Threepenny Opera* by _____ was a big hit in Nazi Germany.

This is an example of a Question 2b or 3b from Section B.

1. Using Source F and your own knowledge, explain how art and culture in Germany changed under the Nazis. **(8 marks)**

Answers online

Source F: *A 1938 painting by Arthur Kampf that commemorated the Nazi seizure of power on 30 January 1933*

The success of Nazi propaganda

Revised

Propaganda is the organised spreading of information which is intended to make people think or act in a certain way. Hitler and the Nazis used propaganda to gain and maintain power.

Films – films and newsreels censored by Goebbels.

Events – dramatic rallies at Nuremberg, and the 1936 Olympics.

Art – art had to show German heroes and family and to be easy to understand.

Radio – cheap radios made but no foreign stations to be listened to.

Books – banned books were burned.

Architecture – public buildings were grand like those in Ancient Greece or Rome.

Newspapers – all supported the Nazis and were told what to print.

> **Revision tip**
>
> This visual aid should help you remember the seven examples of Nazi propaganda.
>
>

Radio: The most important new tool of Nazi propaganda

- The Nazis set up factories to build cheap radios like the 'people's receiver' (*Volksempfänger*) which cost only 35 Reich marks.
- They made sure that the new radios had a limited range so they would only pick up the German stations.
- By 1939, 70 per cent of German households had a radio.
- Loudspeakers were put in factories, cafes, offices, restaurants and even in the streets.
- Listening to foreign radio stations was banned.

Controlling German newspapers

- The Nazis used their own publishing company – Eher Verlag – to gain ownership of newspapers by taking them over.
- On 3 October 1933 the Nazis passed the **'Editors' Law'** which reduced the power of the newspaper owners and gave the editors responsibility for what went into the newspaper.
- In 1932 Nazi newspapers were 2.5 per cent of the total circulation; by 1939 Eher Verlag owned two-thirds of the German press.
- The Propaganda Ministry held daily **press briefings** where journalists were told how detailed articles should be, how events were to be treated and even the size of the headlines.
- The journalists' organisation elected the **Nazi Press Chief**, Otto Dietrich, as their president in 1933 and he made the decisions about who could become a journalist. By 1935, 1300 Jewish and Communist journalists had been sacked.
- Goebbels made sure that the press gave maximum publicity to specially created Nazi events like the Führer's birthday, remembrance of the Munich Putsch in 1923, and the annual Nuremberg rally.

The cult of the Führer

Nazi propaganda worked hard to show Hitler as Germany's saviour. He was shown as a hard worker with few personal pleasures. Many Germans could **identify** with him – the soldiers, farmers and workers could all find something in his past or his promises which appealed to them and made them support him. Anything that they disliked or Nazi failures were, they thought, the result of those around Hitler. Hitler was **charismatic** and had a gift for presenting himself to attract support from different groups in Germany. When he spoke in public he could inspire an audience and get them to believe that he had the answers to Germany's problems.

The reasons for successful propaganda

- Nazi propaganda was everywhere; it was in newspapers, books, theatre and music.
- The German people were prevented from hearing things that the Nazis did not wish them to know.
- The HJ and schools were also used to transmit Nazi ideas.
- Germany was watched over by a secret police and people's trust in each other was undermined by rumours and suspicion.
- German people's ability to be critical was blunted and they were frightened to challenge what they were told.
- People talked and behaved as was expected of them. Propaganda was important in supporting the Nazis' hold on the lives of German people.

Key person

Josef Goebbels
- Hitler's propaganda chief.
- He proved himself very skilful at propaganda during the election campaigns of 1930–33. Goebbels had to prevent anything critical of the Nazis being said or written and make sure that German radio, newspapers and the arts all displayed Nazi ideas.
- Goebbels worked hard to promote Adolf Hitler as the saviour of the German nation and a role model for its people.

Revision task

Use the illustration below to identify and label the ways in which the Nazis influenced what people thought.